BARREL FEVER

DAVID SEDARIS

LITTLE, BROWN AND COMPANY

Boston   New York   Toronto   London

First Edition

This book is a work of fiction. Names, characters, places, and incidents are either the product of the author's imagination or, if real, are used fictitiously.

Grateful acknowledgment is made to National Public Radio's "Morning Edition" and to the following publications in which some of these stories and essays were first published: *Discontents,* "Glen's Homophobia Newsletter Vol. 3, No. 2"; *Harper's,* "SantaLand Diaries" and "Diary of a Smoker"; *New American Writing,* "Firestone"; and *NY Press,* "SantaLand Diaries" and "Season's Greetings to Our Friends and Family!!!"

Library of Congress Cataloging-in-Publication Data
Sedaris, David.
    Barrel fever : stories and essays / by David Sedaris. — 1st ed.
      p. cm.
     I. Title.
  PS3569.E314B3   1994
  814'.54 — dc20   94-7611

10 9 8 7 6 5 4 3 2 1

Designed by Barbara Werden

MV-NY

Published simultaneously in Canada by Little, Brown & Company (Canada) Limited

Printed in the United States of America

To my mother, Sharon

Stories

Essays

I WAS ON "Oprah" a while ago, talking about how I used to love too much. Did you see it? The other guests were men who continue to love too much. Those men were in a place I used to be, and I felt sorry for them. I was the guest who went from loving too much to *being* loved too much. Everybody loves me. I'm the most important person in the lives of almost everyone I know and a good number of people I've never even met. I don't say this casually; I'm just pointing out my qualification.

Because I know the issue from both sides, I am constantly asked for advice. People want to know how I did it. They want to know if I can recommend a therapist. How much it

3

will cost, how long it might take to recover. When asked, I tell them, like I'm telling you, that I have never visited a therapist in my life. I worked things out on my own. I don't see it as any great feat. I just looked at the pattern of my life, decided I didn't like it, and changed. The only reason I agreed to appear on Oprah's panel was because I thought her show could use a little sprucing up. Oprah is a fun girl, but you'd never know it from watching that show of hers, that parade of drunks and one-armed welfare cheats. And of course I did it to help people. I try and make an effort whenever I can.

Growing up, my parents were so very into themselves that I got little love and attention. As a result, I would squeeze the life out of everyone I came into contact with. I would scare away my dates on the first night by telling them that this was *it*, the love experience I'd been waiting for. I would plan our futures. Everything we did together held meaning for me and would remain bright in my memory. By the second date, I would arrive at the boyfriend's apartment carrying a suitcase and a few small pieces of furniture so that when I moved in completely I wouldn't have to hire a crew of movers. When these boyfriends became frightened and backed away, I would hire detectives to follow them. I needed to know that they weren't cheating on me. I would love my dates so much that I would become obsessed. I would dress like them, think like them, listen to the records they enjoyed. I would forget about me!

To make a long story short, I finally confronted my parents, who told me that they were only into themselves because they were afraid I might reject them if they loved me as intensely as they pretended to love themselves. They were hurting, too, and remarkably vulnerable. They always knew how special I was, that I had something extra, that I would eventually become a big celebrity who would belong to the entire world and not just to them. And they were right. I can't hate them for being right. I turned my life around and got on with it.

Did you see the show? Chuck Connors and Cyrus Vance were, in my opinion, just making an appearance in order to bolster their sagging careers. But not Patrick Buchanan. Man, I used to think I had it bad! Patrick Buchanan has chased away every boyfriend he's ever had, and he's still doing it. Patrick is a big crier. He somehow latched on to me and he's been calling and crying ever since the show. That's his trademark, crying and threatening suicide if I don't listen. That guy is a complete emotional cripple, but the other panel members didn't seem fit to speak on the subject. E. G. Marshall, for example, would talk about driving past his ex-boyfriend's house and calling him in the middle of the night just to hear his voice. Chuck Connors said he used to shower his boyfriends with costly gifts. He tried to buy their love. Chuck Connors wouldn't recognize love if it were his own hand, and E. G. Marshall if it were both his hands, one down there and the other gently at his throat.

I am in this week's *People* magazine, but not on the cover. Bruce Springsteen is on the cover with whatshername, that flat-faced new wife of his, Patty Scholastica or Scoliosis — something like that. In the article she refers to Bruce as "the Boss" and discusses what she calls his "private side."

If she's calling Bruce "the Boss," I can tell you she knows absolutely nothing about his "private side."

I was the boss when Bruce and I were together. Maybe I should give this Patty person a call and tell her how Bruce needs to have it, give her a few pointers and clear up this "Boss" issue once and for all. Tell her how Bruce groveled and begged for a commitment and how he behaved when I turned him down. I'd said, "What's the use of being a multimillionaire when you walk around dressed like a second-shift welder at U.S. Pipe & Boiler?" Bruce wants to keep in touch with his "people," which is admirable in theory but grotesque when you consider the fact that his "people" consume gasoline, domestic beer, and acne medication in equal amounts.

Bruce took it hard and picked up these women on the rebound. I remember running into that last wife of his, the model, at a party. It was she, I, Morley Safer, and Waylon Jennings. We were waiting for the elevator, and she was saying to Waylon that Bruce had just donated seven figures to charity, and I said, "No matter how much money Bruce gives to charity, I still say he's one of the tightest men I've ever known." It went right over her head, but Morley knew what I was talking about and we shared a smile.

I am in this week's *People* magazine celebrating my love with Charlton Heston. There are pictures of me tossing a pillow into his face, pretending to be caught during a playful spat. You know that we can be real with one another because on the next page there I am standing on tiptoe planting a big kiss on his neck while Burgess Meredith, Bobby Packwood, and some other old queens are standing and applauding in the background. Then I'm in the kitchen flipping pancakes to show I'm capable. I'm walking down the street with Charlton Heston, and then I'm staring out to sea, digging my bare toes deep into the sand, in this week's *People* magazine.

The press is having a field day over the news of my relationship with Mike Tyson. We tried to keep it a secret, but for Mike and me there can be no privacy. Number one, we're good copy; and number two, we just look so damned good together, so perfect, that everyone wants pictures.

Charlton Heston and I are finished, and he's hurt. I can understand that, but to tell you the truth, I can't feel sorry for him. He had started getting on my nerves a long time ago, before the *People* story, before our television special, even before that March of Dimes telethon. Charlton can be manipulative and possessive. It seems to have taken me a long time to realize that all along I was in love with the *old* Charlton Heston, the one who stood before the Primate Court of Justice in *Planet of the Apes*. The one who had his loincloth stripped off by Dr. Zaus and who stood there naked but unafraid. What a terrific ass Charlton Heston used to have, but, like everything else about him, it's nothing like it used to be.

In the papers Charlton is whining about our relationship and how I've hurt him. I'm afraid that unless Charlton learns to keep his mouth shut, he's going to learn the true meaning of the word *hurt*. Mike is very angry at Charlton right now — very, very angry.

Let me say for the record that Mike Tyson, although he showers me with gifts, is *not* paying for my company. I resent the rumors to the contrary. Mike and I are both wealthy, popular men. The public loves us and we love one another. I don't need Mike Tyson's money any more than he needs mine. This is a difficult concept for a lot of people to grasp, people who are perhaps envious of what Mike and I share. This was the case with Charlton Heston, who lost most of his money in a series of bad investments. It's sad. The man is a big star who makes a fortune delivering the Ten Commandments one day, and then loses it all as a silent partner in a Sambo's restaurant chain the next.

Mike and I would gladly give everything we've got in exchange for a little privacy. We would be happy living in a tent, cooking franks over an open fire on the plot of land we bought just outside Reno. Mike Tyson and I are that much in love. It is unfortunate that our celebrity status does not allow us to celebrate that love in public. Since we were spotted holding hands at a Lakers game, all hell has broken loose, and the "just good friends" line has stopped working. None of this is helping Mike's divorce case or my breakup with Charlton, who, I might add, is demanding some kind of a settlement. For the time being, Mike Tyson and I are lying low. It's killing us, but we've had to put our relationship on the back burner.

I accidentally swallowed Mike Tyson's false teeth. I can't believe it! They were gold, but money isn't the issue. Between the two of us, we could buy gold teeth for every man, woman, and child with the gums to accommodate them. It's not the money that bothers me.

It was late, and Mike had taken his teeth out for the evening. He'd put them in a tumbler of water we kept next to our bed. Mike could sleep with his teeth in, but believe me, it was better with them out. We had just finished making very strenuous, very complete love when I reached for that glass of water and drank it down, teeth and all. It was unsettling. The problem was that Mike was planning to have those teeth set into a medallion of commitment for me. He was gracious and forgiving and said that it was no problem, he'd just have some others made. But those teeth were special, his first real gold teeth. Those were the teeth that had torn into all of the exotic meals I had introduced him to. Those were the teeth I polished with my tongue on our first few dates, the teeth that hypnotized me across a candlelit table, the teeth that reflected the lovelight shining in my eyes. I swallowed Mike Tyson's teeth and let him down.

I've been waiting for days, but they still haven't passed. They have to come out sooner or later, don't they? Even if I do find them, I can't expect Mike to put them back in his mouth. That was a big part of our commitment ceremony. I was supposed to reach into my mouth and pull out a rather expensive diamond-studded ID bracelet I'd had made, and Mike was going to reach into his and withdraw the medallion. Mike said, What the hell, it wasn't like his teeth hadn't been up my ass before. But it was the principle of the thing that got me down.

Mike Tyson and I were arguing over what to name the kitten we'd bought. I would have just as soon taken one of the many free kittens that had been offered to us. Everyone wanted to give Mike and me kittens. I thought we might just take one of those, but Mike said no. He wanted the kitten that had captured his heart from a pet shop window the previous week, a white Persian/Himalayan female. I don't care for puffy cats in the first place, and this one, with her flat face, reminded me of whatshername, Bruce's new girlfriend, Patty. But I said, "All right, Mike." I said, "If you want this Persian/Himalayan mix, then that's what we'll get." I can love just about anything on all fours, so I said, "Fine, whatever." Let me say that a longhaired cat is one thing, but a white Persian/Himalayan blend named Pitty Ting is something else altogether.

I'd wanted to name the kitten Sabrina 2. I'd had another cat, my Sabrina, for years before she died. I was used to the name and the connotations it carried in my mind. Mike, though, was adamant about the name Pitty Ting, which was unfair seeing as I hadn't wanted a puffy cat in the first place, especially a white one that would be hard to keep clean. Besides, this was a relationship in which compromise was supposed to be the name of the game. I gave a little, so why couldn't he?

Driving home from the pet store we started to argue. Mike said some pretty rough things and I responded tit for tat. He was driving like a trained seal, all over the road, and the constant swerving was making me sick to my stomach. The kitten was in the backseat, yowling and carrying on like you wouldn't believe. I turned around and told it to shut up, when, out of the corner of my eye, I saw Mike raise his fist. I thought he was threatening another driver or rolling up the window. It all happened so fast. I saw his raised fist, and then again, I guess I didn't see it.

After he hit me, I got out of the car and walked. I've had some physical fights with boyfriends before, Norman Mailer and Peter Jennings to name just a couple, so I'm no stranger to a flaring temper. This time, though, I just walked away. Mike followed me. He drove his car up onto the sidewalk, but I kept walking, pretending not to notice. Then Mike got out of the car and started begging, begging on his knees, and whimpering. I put my hand up to my eye, pretending to wipe away some of the blood, and then, boy, did I clip him!

While he was unconscious, I let the kitten out of the car and sort of kicked her on her way, no problem. A puffy cat like that will have no problem finding someone to love her. When he came to, Mike had forgotten the entire incident. That happens all the time — he forgets. He didn't even ask why we were spattered with blood. He asked, "What happened?" and I answered, "Don't you remember? You said you wanted to buy me a pony." So then we purchased a beautiful Shetland pony named Sabrina 2. We forgot about naming things, about anything but our relationship. We rode round and round the block on our pony, who groaned beneath the collective weight of our rich and overwhelming capacity for love and understanding.

Mike Tyson started acting out and it got on my nerves. I can overlook an incident here and there, but Mike started pushing it. For example, one night we were having dinner with Bill and Pat Buckley. Now, I've known Bill and Pat for years. We used to vacation together (we all adore sailing), and I think we understand one another fairly well. Bill and Pat have one of those convenient marriages, an arrangement that allows them to pursue sexual relationships on the side with no hard feelings. I met Bill Buckley back when he was going with Redd Foxx, which was years ago.

Pat had recently broken up with Elizabeth Dole and, unfortunately, decided to employ the sordid details of the breakup as our dinner's conversational centerpiece. This is an old habit of hers. Pour a few drinks into Pat Buckley and she'll tell you everything, whether you want to hear it or not. If forced to take sides in the issue, I'm afraid I'd sympathize with Liz Dole, but Mike felt differently. We were having dinner when Pat started telling us about a few of Liz's rather arcane sexual practices. When Bill suggested she change the subject, Mike hauled off and punched him, breaking his jaw as a matter of fact. Afterwards, Pat Buckley thanked Mike Tyson for breaking her husband's jaw. She said she'd spent the last forty years being patronized by men like Bill Buckley. So what does Mike do? He invites Pat to move in with us! Now, I know what Pat Buckley is really like, and I don't want her living in our house, dragging strange girls in and out at all hours of the night. I've seen Pat Buckley in action. I know about the drinking, the drugs, all of it, so I said, "Miiiikkkkeeee," through my clenched teeth. I kicked him under the table and he kicked back.

Mike Tyson is making an ugly face in the "Newsmakers" section of this week's *Newsweek* magazine, an ugly face directed toward me. I'm not frightened so much as shamed and concerned. In the picture Mike's skin seems sallow and blotchy. He looks like he's been rolling around in an ashtray. Our breakup was hard on him, but whining to the press won't help.

I left as soon as Pat Buckley moved in. I guess Mike thought I would change my mind and welcome her into our lives. I guess Mike was wrong.

Pat Buckley didn't stay long. She was dating Mackenzie Phillips at the time and stayed only three weeks before taking off to Cannes or Rio or someplace. Looking back on it, I can't put all the blame on Pat Buckley. Mike and I had problems before she came along, big problems we would have been forced to deal with sooner or later. I don't want to go into any of the details of our relationship, but I would like to set the record straight and say that there is no truth to the rumors about me and Morley Safer. I resent Mike's accusation that Morley and I are anything more than friends.

I resent Mike Tyson's self-pitying ploys for attention. I resent his suggestion that I was in any way false or insincere. Unlike him, I don't care to dwell on the unpleasant aspects of our relationship. I prefer to remember a time when Mike and I, having finished a simple game of cards, were sitting side by side in comfortable reclining chairs. Mike took my hand in his and began, very gently, to pet my fingers, kissing each one, and addressing them as individuals.

MUSIC FOR LOVERS

ANITA O'DAY was recently interviewed on the radio, on one of the stations I am fond of. She was hooked on drugs for years but claims to have kicked the habit. She told the interviewer that she had taken drugs because she had felt like taking drugs. Then, when she no longer felt like it, she went off to Hawaii, where she was a stranger to drug salesmen. She sounded drunk to me. She said, "My name's O'Day and that's pig latin for money, honey, and plenty of it." She must have been drunk to ramble on like that. She claimed that her record company is managed and financed by her dog. Drunk.

It turns out that Anita O'Day is missing her uvula, that sack of flesh that hangs from the rear of most everyone's palate. Hers was accidentally removed during a child-hood tonsillectomy. She was young then and has adjusted, made quite a name for herself.

I've heard Anita O'Day sing plenty of times before but was very excited when, at the end of the interview, the station played a few of her songs. It sounded completely new to me, knowing that she was missing her uvula. Apparently, along with the appendix and tonsils, the uvula is one of those things that we can do without. Since the interview, I cannot get it out of my mind, the idea of this extra baggage. It makes me gag, but still I find myself constantly poking at my uvula with whatever is handy. It's funny. I just want to take a pair of scissors and snip the damned thing off. It would bleed like the devil but it wouldn't kill me.

I am not a physician but have read enough to know that everything is not as complicated as it is made to sound. Most of it is just common sense. For example, I have given my daughter, Dawn, stitches several times. If you can sew a button on a shirt, then you can give someone stitches. Just make sure to use a clean, sharp needle and some strong thread. I recommend un-waxed dental floss. Do not, under any circumstances, use yarn. I found myself in a pinch last year and Dawn still blames me for that scar on her forehead. I said then and I will say now that there is no way I'm going to pay some doctor three hundred dollars just because my daughter got drunk and fell. She certainly doesn't have that kind of money, and whoever it was that pushed her didn't step forward and offer to pay. I am still making payments on the last hospital visit. I will probably be paying on that for the rest of her life. Doctors, hospitals, and insurance companies. The less we have to do with those people the better off we'll be. They have everything very neatly tied up and plan to keep it that way.

Two years ago, when Dawn was fifteen, she fell off the roof. Don't look at me. I have no idea what she was doing up there. I thank God that she landed on her feet. I found her staggering across the lawn and was troubled by her ankles. They felt puffy to me so I set them and applied two fine casts, which, it turned out, were a little bit too tight. Eventually I was forced to carry her to the hospital, where some power-hungry surgeon decided that he needed to amputate both her feet. I am still convinced that her feet were that color not because of gangrene but because they were dirty. Whose feet wouldn't be dirty after three weeks in a cast?

Anita O'Day is the first music I have listened to since I got rid of the stereo. I still have a bit of tissue lodged in my ear. I had to put it there to blot out the new music Dawn was listening to. The paper is lodged way up in the canal and I don't dare try and dig it out myself. Everyone says, "Don't stick sharp objects in your ear." I believe that this is sound advice (ha, ha). Seriously, though, the ear is a complex and delicate thing. My ears are, anyway.

Lately I find myself wishing that, instead of paper, it was a scrap of metal inside my ear. That way I could draw it out using a powerful magnet held up against the side of my head. It would make a satisfying sound when it hit the magnet. Clink!

When I listen to music I like to relax and imagine my place in it. I believe that this is fairly common. I like to imagine myself as the vocalist or, if the singer is a woman, I pretend that I wrote the song and play all of the important instrumental solos. I generally don't listen to music on the radio. It doesn't allow me the time I need to set the stage for myself. I like to know, for instance, where it is that I am performing. How many people are in the audience? What sort of a crowd do they make? As a rule I picture myself playing small clubs where the audience is not allowed to drink or move about freely during my set. They ruin my concentration with their damned tinklings. I almost always imagine Carol, my ex-wife and Dawn's mother, making an appearance during my nightclub act. Sometimes I allow her to stand shivering in the doorway until the end of my set, when she rushes toward me begging forgiveness. The trouble with this is that Carol wouldn't be caught dead drifting into any of the clubs

I fantasize playing. She doesn't give a damn for ballads, for anything that isn't fast and dancey.

It all becomes very complicated and tiresome to imagine, so I rarely listen to music anymore. I do, however, pay close attention to the radio and have quite an impressive collection of tapes. I have the entire Iran-Contra hearings on high-quality Maxell. I tried to draw Dawn into the hearings but she wasn't interested. Daniel Inouye is missing one of his arms and that certainly didn't slow him down or keep him off the radio! I have a complete three-year collection of National Press Club broadcasts along with several hard-to-find Noel Proctor commentaries. I have tapes of myself calling in on "Larry King Live!" and speaking personally to such guests as Ed Meese, Tommy Smothers, Bob Hope, and Jim Brady both before *and* after the accident. Which was the better conversation? *You* be the judge. The local radio hosts can recognize me by voice, and respect the way I have of challenging their guests. It isn't easy getting through to any of these shows, but if you are persistent and have something to say, then you'll find a way to voice your opinion.

I often try and encourage Dawn to call a few shows and speak her mind about the issues. Stupid me, waste of time. Dawn doesn't even know what the issues are. She would sit glued to the television set or else she'd try and hog the phone, making calls to her so-called friends. I sometimes just want to shake the life out of her, to point at the radio waves in the night sky and tell her that, Goddamn it, people are thinking out there.

After I got rid of the TV set Dawn took to listening to a lot of rock music. I can't remember the names of any of the bands. It was just one long, horrible record to me. All of those Englishmen with their weary voices remind me of someone walking very slowly through the garbage they have strewn over the face of this earth. Dawn would sit in her chair and listen to these records, one right after another, which was just not healthy. It is music that was popular during the time she spent dating a boy named Rusty Miller. She used to carry on and on about Rusty. The sun rose and set with him. Rusty wasn't the right type for Dawn but she, of course, couldn't, wouldn't, see it. In my opinion he paid too much attention to his hair. It was sprayed up on top and fell to his shoulders. Beautiful hair, like a girl's. Dawn's hair should look so good. She threatened more than once to run off with this Rusty character. Dramatic. She tried to convince me that she was pregnant with his child and that they would have to get married. They would cross state lines to do it. I knew she was lying. I have a better chance of getting pregnant than she does, but I said, "Fine, all right, you make your filthy bed and you lie in it." But where was Miller after my daughter lost her feet? You tell me. He was just a fair-weather friend and I tell her it's a good thing she found out before it was too late. I found that out about Carol too late. I said, "Look at me."

I figured Dawn had taken up with someone else when she started playing this new music. She hears it on the radio and has gotten hold of some records, too, big 45s the size of regular LPs. These are songs that have been retouched so that the singers stutter and the music falls back on itself. The same lines repeated over and over again as though they were intended for memorization. Simple, stupid lyrics repeated over and over again. "I I I I I II, I Need, I Need You." It's as though the record were scratched intentionally. Normal, thinking people might ask themselves, "Haven't I heard that phrase already?" They might notice that this relentless repetition is, at best, redundant and, at its worst, an insult to one's ability to concentrate on anything of value. Dawn says that the beat is good to dance to. Dance? Her? I say, "Excuse me for nit-picking, but doesn't one need to have two feet in order to dance?" This music encourages her to live in a fantasy world where everything is rosy and brightly possible — no need to work, just sit back and dream, dream your life away.

She's getting these records from some kid down the block. I've seen him around a few times on the street barefoot and shirtless but with a big hairbrush sticking out of his gym shorts. He's not going anyplace barefoot so what does he need with a hairbrush? He's just begging to step on a nail or on some of the broken glass I've set outside Dawn's window and I can't wait until he does.

The songs Dawn played gave me a headache, gave us both a headache. Mine went away after I placed the record player on a high shelf in my bedroom. There's no way Dawn can reach that shelf. I, personally, have to use the stepladder, which suits me fine because it forces me to work for the music I once took for granted. When Dawn's headaches persisted I figured it probably had something to do with her wisdom teeth. Do you have any idea how much it costs to have wisdom teeth removed by a dentist? I've done some research and the procedure is really not as complicated as you might think. I can handle it. Those teeth have to go. If left untended, they could work their way through her skull and into her brain, wiping out every decent idea she might be capable of.

THE LAST YOU'LL HEAR FROM ME

DEAR Friends and Family,

By the time you receive this letter I will be dead. Those of you attending this service are sitting quietly, holding a beautiful paperweight, a gift from the collection, which, in life, had been my pride and joy. You turn the paperweight over in your hands, look deep inside, at the object imbedded in the glass, be it a rose or a scorpion, whatever, and through your tears you ask, "What is death like?" By this time I certainly know the answer to that question but am unable to give details. Know only that I will one day meet you upon the grassy plains of Heaven, where, with the exception of Randy Sykes and Annette Kelper, I will be tickled to embrace you and catch up on all the news. When the time comes I probably won't be too thrilled to see my mother either, but we'll just have to cross that bridge when we come to it.

If my instructions were followed the way I wanted them to be (see attached instruction envelope #1), this letter is being read to you from the pulpit of The Simple Shepherd Church of Christ by my best friend, Eileen Mickey (Hi, Eileen), who is wearing the long-sleeved Lisa Montino designer dress I left behind that always looked so good on me. (Eileen, I hope you either lost some weight or took it out some on the sides or you're not going to be able to breathe. Also, remember it needs to be dry-cleaned. I know how you and your family love to skimp, but please, don't listen to what anyone says about Woolite. Dry-clean!)

Most of you are probably wondering why I did it. You're asking yourselves over and over again, "What could have driven Trish Moody to do such a thing?"

You're whispering, "Why, Lord? Why take Trish Moody? Trish was a ray of bright sunshine, always doing things for other people, always so up and perky and full of love. Pretty too. Just as smart and sweet and pretty as they come."

You're probably shaking your heads and thinking there's plenty of people a lot worse than Trish Moody. There's her former excuse for a boyfriend, Randy Sykes, for example. The boyfriend who, after Trish accidentally backed her car over his dog, practically beat her senseless. He beat her with words but still, it might as well have been with his fists. He struck her again and again with words and names such as "manipulative," "jealous," "childish," and others I wouldn't justify in print. The dog's death was a tragic accident but perhaps also a blessing in disguise as Randy tended to spend entirely too much time with it. The dog was in danger of becoming, like Randy himself, spoiled and disobedient. Besides that, being a registered breed it was headed for unavoidable future hip problems.

What did Trish's mother say when her daughter, heartbroken over her breakup with Randy, came to her in search of love and understanding?

"If you're looking for sympathy you can find it between shit and syphilis in the dictionary."

Perhaps my mother can live with slogans such as this. I know I can't.

Neither can I live surrounded by "friends" such as Annette Kelper. Poor, chubby Annette Kelper, who desperately tries to pretend that nobody notices the fact that she's balding on top of her head. That's right. Look closely — balding just like a man. Perhaps Randy feels sorry for chrome-dome Annette. Maybe that's why he was seen twice in her company in a single five-day period. Seen standing together in the parking lot of the Burger Tabernacle (her home away from home) and seen huddled together, laughing on the escalator of the Crabtree Valley Mall. Annette, my supposed best friend, who secretly wanted and coveted everything I owned. Annette, always in my corner, the balding, chubby girl who said to me, in the spirit of friendship, "You've got to loosen up a little, Trish. People aren't things that you can own and control and arrange to stay a certain way." I remember she said it to me in the bedroom of my own home, her hand on my shoulder, facing left so that I could clearly see how those two top teeth of hers are turning brown as a result of a cheap root canal. I remember feeling sorry for her.

Is everyone on earth as two-faced as Annette Kelper? Is everyone as cruel as Randy Sykes? I think not. Most of you, the loved ones I left behind, are simple, devoted people. I urge you now to take a look around the room. Are Randy Sykes and Annette sitting in the audience? Are they shifting uncomfortably in the pew, shielding their faces with the 8½-by-11 photograph of me I had reproduced to serve as a memento of this occasion?

(Eileen, read this part real fast before they have a chance to leave.) Randy Sykes's dick is the size of my little finger and that's when it's hard. And I'm not counting the nail, just the finger! He had sex two times with a boy at Camp Ticonderoga when he was in junior high school. Maybe that explains why he loves it when somebody sticks their finger up his butt. He used to beg me to do that but I refused. I said, "No way, Randy." He used to do it to himself all the time. That's why I never held hands with him. His hands stink! He secretly thinks he looks like Marlon Brando, but take a good look — a young Marlin Perkins is more like it! Maybe that's what he sees in Annette Kelper — he's an animal lover. She used to come to my house crying, her breath smelling a mile off like her uncle's dick. She said he forced her but that's a lie because you don't force whores and that's what she is — a whore. Annette and Randy deserve each other. Dick-Breath and Stinky-Finger riding up and down the escalator at Crabtree Valley, up and down, up and down. Fancy little shit-heads! Look at them, take a good hard look at them. It's their fault I'm dead. They are to blame. I urge you now to take those paperweights and stone them. Release your anger! The Bible says that it's all right to cast the first stone if someone dead is telling you to do it and I'm telling you now, pretend the paper-weights are stones and cast them upon the guilty. I've put aside my savings to pay for damages to the walls and windows. It's money I was saving for my wedding and there's plenty of it so *throw!* Hurt them the way they hurt me! Kill them! No one will hold you responsible. Kill them!

(Eileen, I'm going to allow a few minutes here because it might take a while for certain people to get into the swing of it. Pop in the cassette marked "Stoning" and wait until both Randy and Annette are lifeless. Wait until everyone has finished with their paperweights and then I want you to hand the microphone over to my mother. Watch the way she trembles and stutters and remember every gesture as if you were me.)

MY MANUSCRIPT

O H, CHAD," Mrs. Holt called brightly in her irritating and bright voice. "There's someone here to see you!"

Chad groaned and stepped out of the shower, taking special care to dry his ~~four inch his seven inch his~~ enormous thirteen-and-a-half-inch ~~penis~~ cock. He was a stud — *and he knew it.* His ass was still a little sore from last night's marathon drill sesh with the guys at the auto plant, but other than that he had no complaints. Wearing only a scant towel, he stepped into the kitchen, where he received a gigantic shock at the sight of his entire ~~hideous nosy hateful~~ family surrounded by a dozen naked but heavily armed ~~guys~~ studs.

"SURPRISE!" they all yelled. And

surprised he was!!! Chad had completely forgotten about his birthday. His father stepped forward and handed him an alcohol cocktail. "We thought maybe for once we'd give you exactly what you wanted," the elder Holt said, and everyone laughed in a good-hearted way.

Chad finished his potent highball in one swallow and then he turned his glass upside down, giving the secret signal, which meant for the studs to open fire and kill everyone in the family except for him.

When they finished Chad said, "Thank you, men. You've given me just what I've always wanted," and then stepping over the bodies, Chad and the studs headed toward the master bedroom to begin a ~~great fun filled sexy~~ sexsational orgy that none of them would soon forget!!!!

Last Christmas I received a set of golf clubs that, my father likes to remind me, cost a goddamned fortune. He says that he would give his right arm for such a beautiful set of clubs. The obvious solution would be for him to take the stinking golf clubs and give me what I wanted in the first place. I had asked for a typewriter — I didn't think it was asking for too much. Terry Glassman got one last year and he's the same age as me. Terry used his typewriter to compose dull, misspelled, and unimaginative letters, which he sent to his father in Arizona. I don't blame Dr. Glassman for never responding. When he got bored with it, Terry threw the typewriter off the roof of his house.

In my manuscript, Terry Glassman plays a minor role as an ungrateful and spoiled Boy Scout who learns the meaning of the expression *Hard Times* when he is discovered nude and vulnerable by a group of randy park rangers who prepare him for a merit badge in give and take! Terry should be grateful to appear in my book but, knowing him, he'll probably threaten to sue. That's Terry Glassman all over. Here I've given him a good eight inches and a shot at immortality and he'll turn on me the same way he did last year when I asked him to pose for a few nude sketches. Ingrate.

A few months ago, for my fourteenth birthday, I asked for a portable tape recorder with a discreet suppository-sized microphone; but did I receive one? Of course not! That would be too obvious, to give someone what he wants. My father told me that if I want to listen to music then I should learn to make it myself. Who said anything about music? Dad said that the guy who can play guitar is going to be the life of the party. He's confusing life with death. The real life of the party is flattened beneath the bed, taping actual sex encounters, not sitting cross-legged on the floor with a guitar, embarrassing himself and others.

I took guitar lessons for two months from Mr. Chatam, an actual midget who teaches at Instrument City over at Northgate Plaza. Mr. Chatam sat perched on the edge of a footstool and wore outfits that a child might wear: checkered suits with clip-on ties and buckled shoes. The guitar was huge in his lap and I would almost feel sorry for him until he opened his wee mouth to say something stupid like "Here's a little number those girlfriends of yours might enjoy hearing!" and he'd force me to follow along as he played another tiresome ballad from something called *The Young Person's Contemporary Songbook*.

In my manuscript, Mr. Chatam is kept in an orphanage, completely nude, his head and body shaved bald, until he is adopted by a group of truck-driving studs for use as a sex baby. Unlike most babies, Mr. Chatam just loves getting spanked and once he starts bawling there's only one way to pacify him!

I never touched that damned guitar except during lessons, so last week my father told me I had to quit. Boohoo. I thought he might follow up by threatening to give my guitar to a deserving person who wouldn't look down his nose at such an expensive gift, but no such luck. Instead he bought me a five-record instructional kit and wants me to teach myself. On the record, the guy plays "If I Had a Hammer" and "Kumbaya" and says things like "C'mon now, let's everybody sing along!" Life of the party.

While he was growing up, my father lived under what he likes to describe as "harsh circumstances" in a small, ugly apartment. By harsh circumstances my father means that they had a curtain instead of a bathroom door. He never had a bedroom and had to sleep on a back-breaking foldout sofa and go to work before and after school, shining shoes and selling newspapers. He has a point there, that's harsh. Unfortunately, they never gave him a medal for it and as a result he brings it up time and time again.

On the way home from my final guitar lesson my father started in once more, telling me how lucky I am. I was thinking that he should spend an hour playing "Up, Up, and Away" while locked in a windowless room with a midget before he came to me talking about luck. What does he know? During the depression, both of my parents had relatives who would crawl out of the woodwork to stay with my grandparents. They were just freeloaders but, in their own way, they made an impression. Picking me up after my last lesson my father told me a story about the longest freeloader, a guy who was studying to become a Greek Orthodox priest. He wasn't a blood relative, but whisper the word *priest* to my grandmother and she'll fall to her knees and cross herself with a speed that betrays her years. So the priest student moved in and slept on the bone-crushing fold-out sofa with my father. This is chock full of possibilities as far as I'm concerned. A freeloader can be just as hot as anyone else. I asked my father what the priest student looked like and he said it wasn't important.

One day, my dad said, he came home from school earlier than usual. Both his parents were at work and he came upon the priest lying upon my grandparent's bed without any pants on. The student did not appear shocked or embarrassed. He told my father that he was just conducting a little experiment. Then he doubled over, held a lit match close to his ass, and farted so that the match flared out. He told my father to lie down beside him and give it a try but, knowing my dad, he didn't. My father said that he couldn't tell his parents, but he knew in that instant that this priest guy was a pogue, a queer. I don't think that lighting farts with a match necessarily makes someone a queer but I went along with it and kept my mouth shut. The flame-thrower stayed on for another three months, during which time my father slept on the hard, cold floor. Hearing of some genuine blood relatives with more money and a spare bedroom, the priest moved on and they never heard from him again. My father told me all this while we were in the car. He usually doesn't talk at all but he had this timed perfectly. He paused at the top of the driveway and turned to me asking, "Have you ever met anyone like that?"

And I said, "What, a priest?"

Goddamn her! Mrs. Peacock has been talking and my parents have decided to listen. This brings my mother and father down several more notches, which is not good, as they have been in the negative column for quite some time. Listening to Mrs. Peacock is like trying to decipher what a groundhog might mean when it clicks its tongue three times and paws at the earth with a hind foot. Mrs. Peacock's thoughts and actions might be of interest to a group of behavioral scientists in search of the missing link, but other than that the woman is worthless and I rue the day she forcibly entered my life.

When my brother was born I told my parents that, while I was very happy for them, I would not, under any circumstances, share my room. I have always had my own room and I plan to keep it that way. My mother is always barging in to say, "Why don't you brighten things up in here, put up a few posters and add a little life?" My mother would not care for any of the posters I might enjoy and it is a constant battle to keep my room clear of anything she might refer to as "a little life." I have a small bed, a lamp, a dresser, and a desk. The only thing I lack is a typewriter. I keep my room very clean and always have. I have been making my bed since I was able to walk and am perfectly capable of washing and ironing my own clothes. I can take care of myself and would appreciate the opportunity to do so in an apartment or small house, even a trailer. While they mean well, I have no use for my parents or Mrs. Peacock, the maid hired shortly after my brother was born. She says she's a housekeeper and not a maid, the difference being that a housekeeper is white, while a maid is colored. She quibbles over words. If, as she says, a housekeeper earns more money than a maid, does a whore earn more money than a slut?

I have not liked or trusted Mrs. Peacock from the moment she entered our home. She looks like she just crawled out of a cave — absolutely wild. She is an animal and no white uniform can disguise it. Every now and then she'll be playing around with my brother, wasting time, and she'll get up close to his face and say, "I'm gonna eat you! Yes, I am, I'm gonna eat you up," which scares the life out of him because it seems entirely possible.

On her second day of work Mrs. Peacock barged into my room uninvited and ripped the covers off the bed, which I was currently, happily, occupying. Fortunately I was wearing pajama bottoms, but how was she to know that? She does the same thing to my sisters, but they don't seem to mind as they are willing to suffer any indignity in order to have someone make their beds.

I put a neatly lettered sign upon my bedroom door reading, "If you can read this message you are already too close. Go away. Iron, sweep the driveway, polish the car, or empty the dishwasher, but leave this room alone." My sign did no good, probably because she can't even read. I should have set steel-jawed leg traps or rigged a bucket of battery acid over the door, seeing as nothing but brute force will keep this hunting-and-gathering primate out of my private domain. The first time Mrs. Peacock violated my privacy she rifled through my dresser drawers and came away with an old summer camp T-shirt I use for . . . testing ideas for my manuscript. I refer to it, in print, as my fantasy rag. I came home from school and she had the nerve to confront me with it. She held it in her dimpled hands as far away from her bloated body as her arms could reach.

"What's this?" she says to me, waving the stiff T-shirt before my eyes. I took issue with this and told her that she knows damned well what it is, anyone with five children should know semen when they see it. She goes, "I never . . ." as if her children were not made by human contact but found beneath one of the tires lying in her yard. I took my property out of her hands and told her that if I ever catch her in my bedroom again I will sue her for unlawful entry and then, just for the fun of it, I will hunt her down and crush her empty skull. She slapped me. I couldn't believe it. She caught me when my guard was down and it still hurts to sleep on the left side of my face. "Nobody has ever talked to me like that," she said.

Nobody? In my book, all the sensible women have gone off to live in Europe and Mrs. Peacock is the only female left in the United States of America. This initially excites her because she is a nymphomaniac slut who looks forward to fucking and sucking her way from Maine to California. Unfortunately for her, though, her dreams will not be realized. Left with no alternative but her, each and every man in America becomes an insatiable homosexual whom I alone can control to do my bidding. They are slaves to their own desire and to me. I order two dozen of my nude and muscular workers to carry Mrs. Peacock off to The Chad Holt (that is my name in the book) Museum of Natural History, where she is put on permanent display as an odd and ugly specimen, reflecting a brutal, bygone world that no longer exists.

I thought about including my mother in the display but decided on sending her to Europe with the rest of her tribe. In her own way she tries, but again and again her mouth gets in the way.

A few days ago I received an emergency page at school, a yellow slip. A yellow slip usually means either death or destruction. I am not terribly attached to anyone in my family, and my parents are heavily insured, so on the way to the office I tried to look on the bright side. It was my mother on the phone calling to say that Mrs. Peacock had found some blood in my underpants. I can't believe that. Those underpants were in a paper bag at the very bottom of the garbage can. I thought they would be safely destroyed, but Mrs. Peacock must have gone through the trash before the garbage studs came to take it away. She goes through everything. "You're not going to throw this away, are you?" she says, and she'll be talking about the grains of rice in the bottom of the salt shaker. "No, Mrs. Peacock, by all means, you take them. They'll come in handy when your son gets out of prison and marries your niece." She doesn't want these things, not really. Her trick is to act like she's happy with any little scrap. She does it to make us look bad and so that my parents will feel sorry for her. I can't believe she made such a big deal out of those underpants.

On the phone I told my mother that some guys at school had been horsing around, putting raw chicken livers in the seats of the brightest students and that I had sat on one. It sounded like a logical story to me. Those assholes in the eighth grade are capable of anything stupid and petty. In my manuscript, though, I have made them capable of anything — period! I could just kick myself for not burning those underpants, and isn't it a shame that it's come to that, having to burn things? It started bleeding back there a few weeks ago, but I have it under control now.

While the imagination certainly has its place, I feel that it is important for a writer to back certain chapters with a little experience, so a few months ago I started hanging out in the rest room of JCPenney in hopes of getting just that — a little experience.

I stood at the urinal for almost two hours before someone finally took the bait and gave me a signal that he was there to play hardball. Meeting his eyes I understood that I could use him as my research stud, fodder for my manuscript — a little footnote who would drive my future biographers wild and leave my readers breathless and hungry for more. Research Stud and I skipped over all of the bullshit that everyone else goes through: the formal introductions, the phone calls, the dates — we just got to the exclamation point right there in the stall! Afterwards, he sort of ruined everything by telling me that he is a political science major at N.C. state and his name is Julian. I hate that name. In my manuscript he is named Dirk. I've made him about three inches taller and have given him a good, thick ten and one-half inches between his legs. Julian and I met in the rest room a few more times before we were interrupted by a store detective who, I am convinced, was interested in arranging a three-way. After that, we started doing it in Julian's car. He'd drive us out into the country and park behind an abandoned house set on a dirt road.

Julian was all right, but nothing at all like the hard-driving top man I've made him out to be in my manuscript. He was actually very stiff and uptight. We'd be doing it and I would whisper, "Talk to me, talk to me," and he'd start telling me about his summer job as a page at the state legislature building. That was not the kind of talk I was after. I asked him if he had any friends he could invite along the next time. I wanted a good mental picture of what it might be like with three or four studs at one time, ramming away and taking it all. When Julian backed off, I went to the bathroom at the Trailways station and found some real men who could help me.

Research Studs numbers five and six were absolute horses. I'm not changing anything about them. My readers are going to get the unbridled truth as far as those cocksmen are concerned. I just wasn't prepared for the bleeding back there. Not buckets of blood but a slow and steady flow that lasted about five days, during which time I considered asking one of my sisters for a tampon.

When my father brought up the priest I had a sinking feeling that something was up, that he knew more than he was letting on. It is confusing when a stupid man plays dumb.

I'll go out later tonight with a flashlight and check to see if my manuscript is still there, out behind the shed, where I keep it buried.

FIRESTONE

AS A favor to my pastor, Carlton Manning has hired me to work at his service station even though I am unable to drive. You might say that this is like having a bald-headed barber or a toothless dentist bending over your body with advice. You might say, "What does he know?" I will bet that he knows more than you think. I bet that he has a great deal of respect and admiration for the teeth you take for granted. Listen to him. He has inside information.

Sometimes I walk to work but usually I take the bus. Many people ride the bus because their own cars are broken or unreliable. These people see me in my uniform and they think Lord knows what, but they act like there is a doctor in the house.

Carlton says that they are looking for free advice. Since I have no knowledge of the automobile, either foreign or domesticated, I reshape their questions into a way that will allow me to fellowship, to make friends out of strangers.

I have made several fine friends on the bus. Friends in need: In need of a dollar or two, in need of a comb, in need of my transistor radio. Last week I gave a woman my sneakers after hearing that vandals had slashed and shredded the seat of her son's motorcycle. Having nothing upon which to sit, her son is forced to walk back and forth between his home and the church where he takes his meals.

"What can I do to help?" I asked myself. "I have no tailoring skills with which to repair a torn motorcycle seat. What can I do?"

"What can you do? Give her your shoes," came the reply from somewhere deep inside my heart.

So I did. I gave her my shoes.

"What do I want with these?" the woman asked.

"That will be revealed in time," I responded.

Now every time I see this woman I ask, "Has it been revealed yet?" She tells me it hasn't but when it is I will be the first to know.

Friends! Every day the bus driver offers me the steering wheel and every day I am forced to turn him down. While I would enjoy nothing more than to shepherd these passengers to their destination I am forced by state and federal law to decline his kind invitation.

I can't drive because of my eyes, which grow weaker by the day. In the future I will be rendered blind by the hand of fate. My poor sight is genital in nature, passed down to me from my mother. I have turned my back against any number of "operations" because I cannot be so presumptuous as to force the hand of God in another direction. I will travel willingly along the path He has designed for me. Whether I walk or stumble or crawl, it is up to Him, not me. Carlton has trouble understanding my position. He says that, in a year or two, he will be in the market for a new liver. He always asks pretty girls if they have one they can spare. Carlton says that he will ask for their livers and steal their hearts while he's at it.

On the radio I hear about men whose time has come, yet they deny the truth and attempt to live off plastic hearts installed in their cut-open chests. But what kind of a life is that, to push your heart's battery over the rugged terrain of this earth? God looks down upon these men who try to wheedle Him out of His plan and I believe He chuckles. He lets them have their minute in the sun and then He calls them up for a consultation. The Lord gives these men just enough rope to hang themselves but in a gentle and crafty way that nobody can imitate or ignore.

Being a very quick learner I took only a few weeks to master my position as a service station attendant. The first hardship was finding the gas tanks, which are designed by hotshots to blend into the surface of the automobile.

Why?

I cannot answer that question. I can only speculate. Perhaps these hotshots would like to convince you that an automobile runs of its own accord, like an animal charging from place to place. You might look at, say, a dog running alongside the road and ask yourself why it runs. Rarely would you ask how the dog runs. You never think of the dog's gas tank, a bowl of food and water set beside his cushion. These hotshots would like to confuse the natural and the mechanical world.

Can they fool the public at large?

Perhaps.

Can they fool me?

No.

Once I located the tanks I found it difficult to read the meter and administer gasoline at the same time.

"Give me seven bucks' worth, unleaded," a customer might say.

"What does that feel like?" I would ask myself. Seven dollars' worth of unleaded gasoline passes quickly. It is a brief period of time compared to the seven dollars' worth one might get from a movie or the time it might take to enjoy a meal at your favorite restaurant. Think about it!

Though my sight is poor I could clearly see that many of the station's visitors were in need of more than gasoline. It was difficult to converse from my position at the rear of the car but where there's a will there is a way. During the chilly weeks of April I found myself hoarse by noon, raising my voice over the sounds of traffic and of life itself. I would minister to all my customers and found the greatest challenge in certain young people who seemed to believe that Hell is nothing more than a hot day at the beach. I would have been more than happy to counsel these people, one on one. If it were to take me the rest of my life I would have accepted the challenge. Sadly, the majority of them refused my offer of guidance.

"F——k you," they would say. "To Hell with your ways, mole."

Without paying they would cut out of the station and squeal their tires onto the busy street, playing their radios so loudly that I could hear them off in the distance for blocks. I would shout after them. I happen to know that Hell is nothing like the beach. There is no sand in Hell, or water either. It is so hot in Hell that the sand has melted. Think about that!

Many people would speak to me about troubles with their cars. They would feel a pull in the steering wheel or hear a noise like someone trapped under the hood was patiently tapping to be let out. Carlton told me to tell them that it sounded like a transmission problem and that they should make an appointment to have one of our men look it over. I understood that this was Carlton's plan to entrap people by making the most of their fears. After the third week I told him that I could no longer be party to that. He did not seem angry or surprised but suggested that I might enjoy a job that gave me more solitude.

I began to work shorter hours on a later shift, a hands-on job designed to acquaint me with humility. I cleaned the rest rooms and found unspeakable things there. Men would advertise themselves on the walls with markers and sharp knives. Carlton had the door taken off the men's room stall when he discovered it was being used as a perverse clubhouse by confused and lonely men. I would mop the floor and clean the sink and toilet daily. "Human waste is, above all, human," I told myself. "I am a human, they are humans." Together we are a humanity who might take a moment or two to clean up after ourselves.

The women were just as bad as the men, sometimes worse. Frightened of germs, many women would use hand towels and toilet paper to fashion a nest upon which to sit. The bathroom floor was a fire hazard. I found quite a few articles of clothing in the women's bathroom. It is I who was responsible for organizing the lost-and-found box at our station. So far, nobody has stepped forward to claim anything so I am considering donating these clothes to the needy. A newborn baby was found at a Sunoco station on Glenwood Avenue last year. It was a baby girl, still alive. She was taken to the hospital and named for a letter of the alphabet. After a month, the mother stepped forward to claim her child.

The mother said that it was a misunderstanding. She said she would never again ask her boyfriend to baby-sit. So how did her boyfriend sneak a baby into the women's rest room? That is what the public wants to know. I have been following the case closely, which is a coincidence because I thought I had discovered a tiny baby in the women's rest room of our station just last week. I followed my instincts and called the police, an ambulance, and Pastor Holden. The moments passed like hours and, in my impatience I reached into the toilet and pulled the baby shape out, thinking it might still be alive, praying I might save it. Thank God I was mistaken. It was not a baby after all. (But it certainly was big enough!)

Following that episode Carlton decided that Taylor should clean the rest rooms, seeing that he has a family to support and is in need of the extra hours. He also assigned Taylor the job of carrying in the beach balls and quarts of Pepsi we offer as premiums to customers who spend twenty dollars or more. In all honesty I felt slightly envious. Here Taylor was, getting all of the good jobs (so I thought). While it was true that he had a child to support, it is also true that the child is twenty-seven years old and currently resides in Feeny State Penitentiary, where he is serving a five-year sentence for armed robbery. It turns out that he robbed a service station. Carlton knows nothing about it. He has been told that Taylor's son is a five-year-old in need of costly rhinoplasty, which will hopefully correct the child's breathing disorder.

"How's the boy?" Carlton might ask.

"Not good, not at all good," Taylor will answer. "Had me up all night long for the past three days. Sounds like somebody scraping a shovel against the pavement. That's exactly what it sounds like, listening to that baby try and grab a breath. It's a sound to break a man's heart."

Taylor told me later that a shovel striking pavement is the sound his sister makes as she snores beside him in bed. It is wrong to lie to Carlton, and I have spent many long hours mulling it over in my mind. If Carlton should come to me and ask, "Is Taylor's son an infant or is he a convict?" I would feel honor-bound to tell the truth. So far he has never asked but, should he, I am prepared to deliver the truth and pray that Taylor will understand.

My next job was to clean the area around the dumpster and to carry in the tubes and tires at closing. That is how I got my picture in the newspaper. I was carrying the inner tubes in a stack around me when someone took a snapshot of it. I had memorized the path from the pump island to the garage and was used to walking in the dark so it was no problem for me. I was right there in the evening paper but you could not see my face, just my legs.

Now Carlton wants me to do this every day. I come in at four-thirty and stand in front of the station wearing tubes until six or later. Carlton says that it is an eye-catcher during rush hour and is good for customer relations. While I pace back and forth I can often hear Carlton's loud voice as he jokes with the customers. He says, "I hope it doesn't tire him out," and "Folks, you are looking at the original boob tube." I wish that I could see the people's faces as they look in amazement at me, a man made of inner tubes, a dark tornado that can save them from drowning.

WE GET ALONG

WE'RE washing down the kitchen in the vacant basement apartment, my mother and I. She opens the cabinet beneath the sink and acknowledges the mildew huddled in the damp corners. "I will destroy you," she whispers, slowly fingering the trigger on the can of disinfectant. "You're scum, do you hear me? Scum."

Personally addressing each stain is a telltale sign that my mother is entering her vengeful stage. I turn on the radio hoping to distract her. "Please, no," she says. "Not that, not now." She says it as though I were a suitor trying to work my hand beneath her apron on the first date. That's when I slam my fist against the refrigerator door and say, "Ma, I'm lonely."

It's something I saw someone do last night on TV, a handsome, sunburnt pioneer boy heading west in a soiled Conestoga wagon. In the movie the mother gathered the boy in her arms and stroked his head, offering words of comfort and staring off into the bright horizon that suddenly appeared before her.

In the basement apartment my mother wrings out her sponge and says, "Lonely? You'll find out what lonely is if you don't quit acting like a goddamned monkey and get on the stick. Then you'll see lonely."

A monkey? Bless her heart, my mother thinks I would be lonelier without her.

"You're the man now," she said to me after my father died, "you're the man." Then she turned to Popeye, our calico tom, and said, "You're the cat now, Popeye, you're the cat," as if she'd always worn a veil over her face and had never known we were men and cats all along.

The night after his funeral my mother smashed the Pontiac windows with a golf club. I was in bed watching TV when I heard the noise and came running out barefoot in my robe thinking it was someone, some kids maybe, and there she was standing beside the car with this golf club. The windshield was webbed and sagging, and she stepped back to take another crack at it. There was a moth on her forehead. I took the club from her hands and said, "Mother, listen to me. This is *our* car. Why not the Dinellos' or the Ablemans'?" She said she preferred the Pontiac as she was within the rights of the law to destroy her own property.

Another moth, this one brilliant and spotted, lighted on her shoulder, and we all watched as the windshield heaved and collapsed, raining chunks like crushed ice onto the dash and front seat.

We replaced the windshield with plastic as a temporary measure. I ride shotgun, my head out the window like a dog, while my mother drives slowly, cursing, the cigarette poking out of her mouth like a fuse. The drivers behind us grouse and honk their horns.

"Listen to them," my mother says, tightening her grip on the wheel, "all in a big hurry to meet some big stinking heart attack." It embarrasses me that she cannot recognize herself in others. "The trick is not to allow yourself to be consumed by your anger," she whispers between clenched teeth, her knuckles white. She says she would like to have his body exhumed so she can spit on it.

"That'll cost money."

"We'll go there at night with shovels, just the two of us," she says. "What'll it cost?"

I say, "He's rotting flesh now, and long fingernails. You don't want to see that."

"I would pay dearly to see a thing like that. Name your price."

That was months ago, before she developed her theory that he wasn't really dead at all. During the latter period she spent a great deal of time behaving in a clairvoyant fashion. Placing her index fingers to her temples she would pronounce, "Right this minute he's sitting beside a puddle — no, a pool. I see a swimming pool and a . . . checkered bathing suit, a wet bathing suit. I see a diving board and . . . what's this? I see a cocktail napkin that reads . . . 'Fort Cheswick' — no, I take that back! It reads 'Port Selznick . . . Country Club.' There's something written beneath it . . . something in very tiny letters. . . . I'm seeing the letter H . . . and the letter V and . . ." At this point she would surrender her head to the tabletop. "Goddamn you," she would say. "I've lost it. I was this close, Dale, and then I lost it when you cracked that ice tray."

I would then pour my Pepsi and remind her that we had both seen his body after the accident. We saw his arm torn off at the shoulder and lying in a separate bag beside him.

"He was in a drawer," I'd say. "Normal, healthy adults do not choose to spend their time in a refrigerated morgue. If he had it in him to play this sort of joke, chances are we would have known it before now."

"He lied to me for fifteen years so why should I believe him now? Maybe he's alive with one arm. It happens."

My mother's sister Margery refers to this as "Evelyne's stage of denial." Since my father's death my mother has grown closer to her sister Margery, who provides her with slogans such as "God doesn't close one door without opening another," "One day at a time," and, my mother's favorite, "You're only as sick as your secrets."

I feel sick.

I'm cleaning the refrigerator in the basement apartment when I find two squirrel tails in the crisper and another one, attached to the genuine article, wrapped in newspaper in the freezer. The squirrel looks pathetically eager, its paws frozen beside its terrible, crowded mouth.

"Oh, that Nick Papanides was one sick customer," my mother says, referring to the former tenant. "He and I were standing in the backyard one day last month when Popeye dragged home a squirrel, the way he'll do sometimes — it wasn't quite dead yet. It was putting up a fight but you could tell this one wasn't going to climb any more trees. It was pitiful. We're standing there when Nick asks, 'May I?' So I said, 'Hell, it's a free country — knock yourself out.' Then he throws a towel over the damned thing, stomps on it a few times, and carries it into the apartment. He used to cook them with eggplant," she says. "I can't say I'm too sorry to see him go. You couldn't pay me to eat a goddamned squirrel — it's nothing but a rat with long fingernails and a pretty tail." She pauses to scratch at her ankle with the rough side of a sponge. "There's a type that rents basement apartments," she says. "They need a low ceiling to match their self-esteem. You couldn't *pay* me to live with pipes eight inches over my head. We should try renting out the attic — get some cheerful people around here for a change."

I thought Nick was cheerful enough. He was no Shirley Temple but neither was he the despondent mole my mother would have me believe. Before he moved away, Nick and I would lie upon his big water bed, naked, listening to my mother's voice and footsteps as she paced back and forth with the telephone.

"She is laying each of her cards upon a table tonight," Nick would say.

It killed me, the way he put a phrase together. Instead of "off the deep end," he'd say "into the part where the water is more high than your head."

One way or another you find things out about people. After a tenant leaves, we always find something, objects hidden and forgotten about or just left behind. We've found bottles of pills and birthday cards, cassette tapes and jewelry and pictures drawn on the backs of playing cards. We use these things to put together a better idea of the people we thought we knew.

Tom Dodges, for example, left behind two ink-stained bras, a mason jar of gasoline, a book on ventriloquism, and a pillowcase stuffed with dog hair. Tom Dodges, a grown man! He moved out to attend a technical college and was replaced by a loud, chumpy dope my mother and I refer to as "The Sportsman." The Sportsman worked as a printer and presented me with dozens of single-sheet calendars picturing naked women leaning against motorcycles or bent over the hoods of troubled cars: women holding tools as if they were trophies they had won for being pert and shameless.

"Add this to your collection," he would whisper. After a while I stopped opening them.

The Sportsman was clinically obsessed with any game involving a ball. Any round object that moved along the ground or through the air; smacked with a bat or club, kicked, dribbled, passed by hand or prodded with a cue, mallet, or paddle — it commanded his full attention. He followed all games, either on television or radio, the volume so loud that it could be heard all the way down the street. It was his habit to coach the players from wherever he happened to be. "Cahill, you shithead, what's your problem? Jesus Christ, you couldn't catch a fucking cold.

Hand that uniform over to your mother, why don't you, you faggoty piece of shit."

It got on my nerves in a big way. Even with tissue stuffed into my ears I could still hear him from my bedroom. I made it a point to avoid him, but certain people can't take a clue. The moment I passed his window or open door he would call out, "Hey, Dale, you watching the game?"

"No."

"You're kidding me, right? The *Stallions* are ahead by eight points with twenty minutes left in the game and you mean to tell me you're not watching? What are you, some kind of an apple polisher, running off to polish some goddamned apple?"

He would rapidly rub his hands along the sides of his sweaty beer can, a dopey illustration of the verb *polish*, and then, thankfully, the televised ball would regain his attention and I was able to pass.

The hands-down worst day of my entire life was the October afternoon when the Sportsman took me to an actual football game. He had bought the tickets in advance and arranged everything with my father. I would sooner eat a Vaseline sandwich than witness two minutes of a football game on TV, let alone an actual, live game. I began feigning illness three days in advance, unforgiving chills accompanied by memory loss and a stiffening of the joints. I was in my bedroom, moaning, when the Sportsman arrived at my door, accompanied by my father.

"Who are you and what do you want with me?" I asked, my stiff arms raised against the light. "I'm so cold, so . . . cold. When will it stop being winter? So . . . cold. If you have any decency, sirs, you will leave me alone to die with dignity."

"Get up and get dressed," my father shouted, ripping the blankets from the bed. "Either that or you'll go in your pajamas."

I gave it another shot. "Go? Go where? Are you taking me to the hospital? Will it be warm there? Who are you? Are you one of the soldiers who visited yesterday? I told you, we have no more bread. We've had no bread for weeks."

"Hey, my man," the Sportsman said when I met him a few minutes later on the sidewalk. "Give me five."

We took a bus to the stadium and this bus, it crawled while Mr. Congeniality struck up a game-related conversation with every passenger, all of whom seemed to find him charming. The stadium was even worse. Once the game began, the Sportsman was riveted, screaming and leaping up from his seat, rooting with the best of them. It was a safe bet that he wasn't going anywhere until long after the last ball was mauled. I excused myself and took the next bus home. Nobody was there, so I rooted through the kitchen drawers and found the spare key to the Sportsman's apartment, figuring I would go down and investigate for a while. I've done it with every tenant, and why shouldn't I? It's my house too, partly. I wanted to discover the Sportsman's pathetic secrets: the sheets stained with urine and decorated with hairs, the magazines beside a foul toilet, the medication and letters they all keep.

One time, while Tom Dodges was out of town, I found, beside a shit-smeared pillow, a magazine picturing naked men, women, and children summering at a nudist colony. These people went about their business, picnicking, cycling, enjoying a barbecue — they were just like anyone else except that they were naked. Most of them, the parents, were uninviting in their nudity. I mean, you really wouldn't want to see them that way, but in this magazine you had no choice. Someone, probably Tom, had accentuated this magazine, with a ballpoint pen. The nudists were provided with thoughts and dialogue, crudely contained within cloud-shaped bubbles that poured from their mouths. "You want a nice big hot dog?"

When Tom returned from his vacation I looked at him differently. I acted the same, but in my mind he became a specimen. Every time he greeted me I pictured those nudists and the filthy pillow. I had always liked Tom and my experience in his apartment made a deep impression on me. Any of us could die tomorrow. It happens all the time. Any of us could have our home broken into and examined by thieves. If I can enter a tenant's apartment, who's to say that he can't enter mine? I have learned to destroy all the evidence. It isn't enough to hide it; you have to burn it and trust that the important secrets will be held in your mind.

I entered the Sportsman's apartment because I wanted to see him differently, to see through him with absolute conviction. I felt I deserved the sensation after everything he had put me through. So I went. I let myself in, quietly, and discovered my father and Aunt Margery on the foldout sofa bed. They were actively naked and it took them a moment or two to notice me standing there.

"Jesus," my father said, covering my aunt's face with a sofa cushion.

"Jesus Christ," my aunt said in a muffled voice, struggling against the pillow.

I said, "Oh, Lord."

It strikes me as funny that Jesus' name was invoked at this time and with such sincerity. Jesus, in pictures, has a beard and long, healthy-looking hair. His eyes are moist with pain and compassion, pretty eyes. That is all I know about him, yet, in times of crisis, his seems to be the name that comes to our lips whether we believe or not. In that regard he has a very good reputation. The details of my father's naked body do not bear reporting. When he stood up I looked away. I saw a dress neatly folded upon the TV set, placed beside a bra and panties. I saw my father's pants and briefs, a tangled ball beside the coffee table.

"Jesus," we all said again, in unison. "Jesus Christ."

The Sportsman moved out toward the start of the upcoming baseball season, just before my father died. He left behind an NFL cigarette lighter, a sink full of dirty plastic dishes, three motel bath towels, countless newspapers and magazines, his unused broom and mop, and stickers: team stickers plastered to the windows, the refrigerator, the kitchen cabinets, even the bathtub! It took my mother and me hours with razor blades and lighter fluid to ease them off. The Sportsman left behind a real mess.

My father hadn't planned on dying and left behind everything, including a small notebook hidden in the drawer of his desk at work. It is a child's notebook, the cover decorated with satisfied cartoon bears presenting one another with bright balloons. Inside he stupidly recorded all of the women he had screwed with, their names, the color of their hair, a pathetic, juvenile assessment. In the notebook my mother is never referred to.

He died on a warm spring day when his company car was sideswiped by a Mayflower van. He looked over at the place where his arm used to be and literally died of shock. Many of the names in my father's notebook are familiar. These are women we know from the stores we frequent, from the neighborhood we live in. He died of shock but look at us, carrying on!

My mother was vacuuming the carpet in the basement apartment when she discovered some pictures on the floor of the bedroom closet. She takes her glasses from her smock pocket and holds them before her eyes. "Oh, that Nick Papanides, I had him figured out right from the start. A Greek god on loan from Mount Olympus to the women of America."

I ask to see the pictures and she tells me I am too young.

"Greeks," she says, "Greeks are just Jews without money." Mom is down on the Jews since discovering my father had carried on with Sandy Ableman, a former best friend.

"Honest Ableman," she says, raising her voice over the noise of the vacuum cleaner. "She'd say 'Evelyne, who but your best friend can you rely on for the truth?' Then she'd say, 'And the truth is that you need to cut your hair. You're too old to carry off that length. It might work for a teenager, but face it, Evelyne, you're no teenager. Far from it.' So what did I do? I cut my hair! Then she got honest about my clothing and the shade of yellow I used on the front steps. So I stopped wearing bright colors and repainted the stairs that shit-brown color she recommended. I'd say, 'Oh, thank you, Sandy, thank you,' and all the while she was sneaking around with my husband. She'd say, 'The truth hurts, Evelyne.' The truth! Do you know what I'll say the next time I see her?"

"We can grow your hair back, Mother."

"You know what I'll say the next time I run into that lying whore?"

I know. She'll say the exact same thing she said the last time we ran into Sandy Ableman. She'll say, "Sandy, it's so good to see you." Then Mrs. Ableman will take my mother's hand and say, "Evelyne, I have been meaning to call you. How are you and Dale making out these days?" Then my mother will look at the ground and look at me and say, "We get along."

"You know what I'll do the next time I see that flowering Judas?" My mother lifts the vacuum cleaner by the hose and gives it a violent jerk. It falls to its side, helpless and struggling. Something has been shaken loose, and she stands there, glaring down at the vacuum cleaner, both of them panting.

"Let's take a little break," I say. We've brought a can of Pepsi and a thermos of coffee — a thermos, even though we live right upstairs. The thermos allows us to feel that we've gotten away. I pour her a cup of coffee and hand her a couple of Tums. My mother washes her hands and looks around the room in a panic.

"That Greek bastard, where's the little TV I loaned him? Can you believe this? He stole the television set and I can't even take it out of his security deposit because he never *gave* me a god-damned security deposit. He said, 'Next time, next time,' and I trusted him and he walked off with my TV set. It wasn't much, but it worked. That lousy shit. 'You can't trust anyone' — I'm going to have that tattooed on my hand in capital letters."

She eats her Tums and they seem to have an immediate effect. "What the hell," she says, her lips chalky. "Why let ourselves get so worked up over a black-and-white TV set? The damned thing didn't even have an antenna. Who cares? Let him choke on it. He was garbage just like all the rest of them. And speaking of trash, have you run into that Spacely woman at school lately, your father's favorite brunette?"

"That's Spakey, Mother, and no, I haven't seen her. She's a junior high teacher, and I'm at a different school now, remember?"

"Well, won't she come to your school sooner or later for a PTA meeting or something?"

"She'll have PTA at her own school."

"Well, won't she have to visit your school for some kind of a conference or something?"

I know what she's getting at, so I give up and say, "Yes, sooner or later I guess she will."

"And what are you going to say when you see her?"

This is one of my mother's tests and I have no choice but to satisfy her with an appropriate answer. I take a sip of my Pepsi and stare out the window where I watch the Dinellos' dog squat and void in our front yard. "I'll say, 'Oh, Miss Spakey, that was very nice of you to give me an A in your class. My father only gave you a C-.' "

"You can do a lot better than that," my mother says, lifting the thermos cup to her mouth.

"All right, I'll say, 'Miss Spakey, isn't it ironic that while I was busy adding and subtracting you were dividing and trying to multiply.' " I know this is bad. My cheeks flame. My mother looks away, a kind gesture on her part. "OK, how's this? I'll say, 'By the way, Miss Spakey, are you still teaching math or did they transfer you over to home wreck?' "

My mother laughs, my reward. "Oh, that's rich," she says. "Home wreck, that's very good."

I think it's just OK. Given time, I'm sure I could think of something better but, unlike my mother, I lack the ability to dwell on these vengeful scripts. I do it for her but personally I just don't work that way. I'm certain that, when and if I ever see Miss Spakey again, we will both look away. She was my seventh-grade math teacher. Seventh grade, that was two years ago. Did she sleep with my father while I was her student? Did their union affect my grades? Did she look at me any differently? I, personally, do not care one way or the other. I don't wish her the worst, nor do I wish her the best. I don't wish her period. Her very existence is a mistake, but it is not *my* mistake, so I'd rather not waste my time thinking about it. My mother, on the other hand, can't stop thinking about it. I can practically see the thoughts as they stomp about my mother's skull. They are the size of a cigarette lighter, yet their feet are heavy and dangerous and they give her no peace.

"Have you given any more thought to that W.S.?" she asks.

"W.S." was my father's only initialed blond encounter. "W.S. Blond (today) Sack of Hammers!!!"

My mother went through his address book, his wallet, his file cabinet, and, finding nothing, resorted to the phone book. It's the not knowing that kills her. Unlike the adulteresses she does know, my mother had taken to calling these W.S.'s. She calls and says, "I am the widow of Les Poppins." I listen in on the other phone as they say, "What? Who?" A few of them she has taken to calling very late at night, a dangerous thing to do if you're going to give out your last name.

"I think I've got it narrowed down between Winnona Spears and Wendy Sidawell," she says. "That Spears gal has the nerve to say I'm harassing her — that's a guilty conscience talking. She's cagey that one. On the other hand, we've got Wendy Sidawell, an absolute moron. 'Huh?' she said the first time I called her, 'What is this, some kind of a contest? Are you with the radio? Am I winning something?' They don't come much dumber than Wendy Sidawell. She's just your father's type. I asked her what color her hair is and she said 'The hair on my head?' When I asked Winnona Spears she threatened me with a lawsuit. The two of them are running neck and neck in my book. Which do you think it is?"

I'm spraying the oven and the fumes are making me dizzy. I back away, frightened that I might tell the truth. W.S. Wife's sister — Aunt Margery. Even if I hadn't seen it with my own eyes the "Sack of Hammers" would have given her away. "I still think it was Wanda Sparks," I say. Wanda Sparks was the one W.S. whose phone has been disconnected. "I think that after he died she packed up and left town. I think she's probably living somewhere out west, somewhere in the desert. I think she's maybe in a rehab center, trying to pick up the pieces."

I'd like for my mother to drop the whole thing, forget it, leave it alone. I try to lead her in another direction but I can't stop thinking about Nick. Why would he have taken off with that TV set when he hardly ever watched it? I was always the one to turn it on. Then he would ask me to get up and change the channel, wanting, I guess, to watch me naked and bending over. Perhaps it was just a prop.

"Make the thing stop talking now," he would say. "Only the picture if you want it there."

"The thing to do is to call them both and have *you* listen to their voices," my mother says. "We'll give them a call later tonight, when their guards are down. You call them and say you're Les Poppins's son, then we'll hear what they have to say. Use that little-boy voice of yours while I listen in on the other line. Tell them your father just died and we'll flush them out, the bitches."

I'm bucking for a way out when my mother's sister Margery pops in. That's Margery's word, "popped," as if she's the cork in a bottle of champagne, the symbol of fun. Margery has just returned from an AA meeting. She goes twice a week as a show of strength for her third husband, Chet Wallace, an alcoholic real estate broker. Margery opens the door, "Yoo-hoo!" and she says to me, "Dale, run upstairs and bring your tired old aunt a beer. After three hours of hearing those people whining about it, I need a drink." She removes her coat and shakes it as though she were provoking a bull. "Goddamn, those alcoholics can smoke — quit drinking so they can turn around and die from cancer. I leave those meetings with my clothes stinking like they're woven from cigarette butts." She takes a seat on my mother's folding chair, spreading the coat over herself like a bib. "Are you people cold or is it just me? Jesus, it's cold in here. No wonder you can't keep a tenant. Dale, did I ask you for a beer or did I not?" I love to make her ask me at least twice as it always makes the request sound more desperate: booze, booze, booze, booze. The longest I've held out is five times.

"Dale, go on now, get your aunt a beer," my mother says.

I give Margery my "I have seen you naked" look, but, as always, it has no effect. She studies her coat for lint and says, "Did you hear your mother?" Margery is under the impression that I was set upon this earth to act as her personal slave. This time though, I don't mind.

On my way out the door I grab my mother's smock off the kitchen counter. I wait until I'm in the upstairs bathroom and then I remove the pictures from the pocket. There are three of them, Polaroids. One is a picture of Nick standing proud and naked against a paneled wall. His stomach catches the light. It is pale, covered with thick black hair and it stands out, like something held before him. He's got a drink in one hand and is using the other to point at his flaccid penis, as if it were not a part of himself but some rare, exotic creature briefly resting between his legs. In another picture I see his short, ringed fingers petting a woman's breast. In the third I find a washed-out, horrified woman sitting naked upon an orange bedspread, waving her arms and trying to stop this from happening. The picture is blurred but I identify the woman as Elaine Petrakis, the hostess over at The Golden Key, the restaurant where Nick worked as a cook. I fan the pictures before my face and cast them into the sink, pretending to care. It's a bit like trying to force yourself to vomit. I look up into the mirror and wail, "Nick, Nick how *could* you?" My face looks best when it is screwed into an expression of turmoil — in repose my features tend to come across as flat, like a face painted upon a plate. I examine my tortured self in the mirror and I like what I see — a guy who hurts, who really cares. "Nicky, how could you do this to me? Especially with Elaine Petrakis, the hostess, that same hostess who smiled my way every time I snuck into the restaurant to see you. Nick, you son of a goddamned bitch, don't you know that I love you?"

I force myself to cry and admire the tears upon my cheeks. I watch in the mirror as my hand moves, broadcasting the sorrow across my face. "I loved you. Sweet Jesus, I loved you so much. Hold me. Just hold me."

The perfect moment suddenly turns sour and I find myself embarrassed at the sight of myself. I didn't love him. I do not feel betrayed by the photographs. Rather, I find myself thinking of that squirrel in his freezer, of squirrels baking away in that oven of his, and I say, "Nick, how *could* you? Why didn't anybody tell me?" To eat squirrels that the cat dragged in — that's sick. And to think I ever even thought about kissing him! I mean, I might allow Popeye to lick my face every now and then, but that's different. Popeye only caught the squirrels, he never ate them.

"Nick Papanides," I say, spitting into the sink. "Let me tell you a little something, Mister. You can rot in Hell for all I care. You can . . ." I watch my saliva clinging to the rim of the basin and wonder where the bubbles come from. Is that air or are we all naturally carbonated? If Nick were to appear before me right this moment I might ask him that question but find myself bored with his answer. That's the kind of guy he was. I wouldn't even have thought of asking my father that question as the answer would have been both dull and uninformed, a double whammy of tedium. That was his claim to fame, we all knew it. My mother though, she seems to cling to an idea of this man. She never seemed to want him alive, but dead he assumes a potential for change. His corpse is something to be claimed and fought over while his life, like Nick's, is transparent to a fault. You'd have to be blind, deaf, and dumb not to know what you're getting yourself into, so if there's blame, blame yourself.

It suddenly becomes clear that a cat has more sense than Nick Papanides. I slip the pictures back into my mother's smock pocket and go down to the kitchen where I take Margery's beer out of the refrigerator. I open the can, take a deep swallow, but spit it back into the can. I don't get it, beer — it's nasty tasting. I follow it up with a tug of Pepsi and close the refrigerator, the door of which is decorated with inspirational messages provided by Aunt Margery. There is a bumper sticker reading "Keep It Simple," and a sympathy card reading "You are not alone!" But she is alone, my mother. She just doesn't know it. It's like falling asleep in your bedroom believing that someone else is quietly sitting in the living room. You feel their presence when actually they're not home at all, they're down the block, living it up. But if the false idea of your company helps them to sleep then why tell them otherwise? It's pitiful. You might look upon a child or a simpleton with pity, no problem, but it's ugly work to see your mother that way. It's much more tiring than cleaning an empty apartment or attending a football game. Like seeing my naked father, clumsy, the words pouring out of him like brown water — I never wanted to see him like that. These thoughts become my job and I clock in and out, every day of my life.

I laughed when I heard the news that my father had died. I celebrate his death every time his name is spoken. In my opinion, the driver of the Mayflower van deserves the keys to the city. The hero responsible for Margery's eventual death should have a national holiday named in his or her honor. They should have their head placed on stamps.

I return to the basement apartment and, entering the kitchen, I pretend to trip. My aunt covers her hair with one hand and her coat with the other — unconcerned for my safety but frightened that I might shower her with the stinking beer.

"I swear," she says, recovering herself. "I shouldn't but I do." She settles back into her chair and takes a greedy sip. A golden stream dribbles out of her mouth and falls upon her coat. Margery removes a Kleenex from her purse and, frowning, mops at the stain. "My coat," she whispers.

"You're looking very pretty tonight," my mother says. Margery has spruced herself up since marrying Chet Wallace. She has stopped bleaching her hair and currently wears it cut short and heavily gelled, brushed toward her face. She's wearing heavy red blush, which, combined with her hairstyle, makes her look as though she has just come up for a quick breath while bobbing for apples. She studies her reflection in the dark window and then looks down into her beer.

"So, how is my big old baby sister doing today?" she asks. "I worry about you here all by yourself."

"I've got Dale," my mother says. "He's with me."

Margery pulls her coat close to her neck and says, "I worry about you, I can't help myself. Chet wanted me to go with him to the Angus Barn for dinner, him and his sponsor and a few other people, marvelous people, but I said, 'No, thank you, I've got to check in on that baby sister of mine because I worry about her.' " She takes another sip of her beer and beams.

This is standard Margery, to tell my mother stories of all the sacrifices she's made to be here.

"They all said, 'Margery, come *on!* Come out and have some fun for a change.' They said, 'What is it with this sister of yours?' Then Chet's sponsor, Bobby, said, 'Sister, hell, I believe she's got a man tucked away somewhere on the sly,' and everyone laughed. They simply would *not* leave me alone." Margery paused, shaking her head at the thought of them. "Those people, bless their hearts. They've saved my husband's life and I love them for it, but still I worry about you and that's why I'm here."

"The Angus Barn," my mother says. "Isn't that the place out on Highway 70 where they wheel around the raw steaks and let you choose the one you want? I believe I went there once with Les when Dale was a baby."

"Les this, Les that," Margery says. "Let it go! You're a fool to even speak that man's name. You're allowing him to live rent-free in your head. Now's the time to let go of the past and move on! Look at me, I've moved ahead like you wouldn't believe. If you want my opinion, you're lucky that the man is dead and buried. Divorce is a lot worse than death, trust me. In death you get a lot more money. In divorce you get nothing but the same old promises — that coupled with the chance of running into the fat creep every time you leave the house. Look at me, I ran into my ex-husband just this afternoon, at Clawsons."

"Which one?" I ask.

"The one on Glenwood Avenue," she answers, mocking my voice, high-pitched and acidic.

I meant which ex-husband, and she knows it.

"I ran into Terry Berringer and hardly recognized him. He looks like a snowman except, you know, made out of flesh. That man must have gained himself a good one hundred and fifty pounds since I left him. There he was pushing a cart like a death wish — all of the food was fatty and cancerous. God, that man can shovel it in. Even his eyes have gotten fat." She crosses her legs and dents her empty beer can. "I hope I never get fat eyes like that," she whispers, squinting at her reflection in the dark window.

"I don't think you have anything to worry about, Margery," my mother says. "You've got very slim eyes."

"Everyone tells me I've got pretty eyes," Margery says. "Everyone. They start in with my eyes and work their way down. Eyes are the mirror of your soul; they reflect what's there, that's their job." She places her hands to the side of her face and leans into them, removing the creases. That's the oldest trick in the book, that attempt to appear both young and pensive. You see it all the time in magazines. "Eyes," she says. "I don't know why I even brought them up. Here I am carrying on and on when my problems are nothing compared to yours. Here you are without a pot to pee in, pardon my French, while I'm speaking philosophy."

My mother rubs a washrag into the palm of her hand.

"Dale, run upstairs and get me another beer," Aunt Margery says.

"Another what?"

"Beer," she says. "Can't you understand English — BEER."

"Go upstairs and get you an ear?" I am hoping to break my record.

"Dale," my mother says, "go upstairs and bring your aunt a beer before you drive me to distraction."

So I head upstairs thinking that something is definitely wrong in this world when my aunt can order *me* to fetch the drinks for *her.* It should be the other way around! "You there," I'd say, "bring me a Pepsi in a tall glass with five ice cubes. Now."

"But Master," she'd say, kneeling, "there is no Pepsi left and the nearest store is closed for the evening."

"Then run to the store that *is* open," I would command. "Don't bother me with the logistics — run, woman, run." She should be *my* slave, and yet I am hers.

There is one beer left in the refrigerator. I take it in my hand and dance about the kitchen. I dance the way I see them dance on television, as if I'm on fire. I shake that can and on my way downstairs I toss it from one landing to the next. Standing at the door to the basement apartment I notice that it has begun to snow, the first snowfall of the season. Snow is great that way, the first snowfall of the season and you look at the world as though you'd never seen it before, as if you had forgotten such a thing was possible.

I dart into the apartment, hand Margery the beer, and leave, saying, "Time for my program. I've got to go." Outside, on the landing, I hear Margery say, "That boy watches too much TV if you ask me. He should be involved in sports or homework or something. It's not good for him, all this television. Ivey Ingers's son watched too much television and look what happened to him! He'll be in prison for the rest of his life."

"Dale's not that way," my mother says.

"That's what Ivey Ingers thought before the trial," Margery says. "Here she is, her only son ties naked ten-year-old girls to trees and she's on TV saying, 'He's not so bad.' "

I am waiting for the explosion. Margery rarely opens a beer while she is preaching. During her lectures she taps the can with her fingers as if the beer is her brain and she is prodding it for wisdom. Both of them are silent and it is getting late. In a moment or two my mother will say, "Stay for dinner, Margery. I'll cook something nice."

Then Margery will say thanks, but no thanks. She'll say that Chet is feeding her leftovers from the Angus Barn. She just popped in, she'll say. Just a quick yoo-hoo! She's sorry but she'll have to leave right after this beer.

Standing outside the door I press my head against the mailbox and wish that she might stay, knowing that, following her beer bomb departure, my mother and I will make certain phone calls. She'll listen in on the other line as I dial and soften my voice, identifying myself as the son of a man named Les Poppins. I will hear my mother's measured breath from the next room as these women, sleepy and innocent, whisper, "What? Who? Why do you keep calling me? Why can't you leave me alone?"

GLEN'S HOMOPHOBIA
NEWSLETTER VOL. 3, NO. 2

DEAR Subscriber,

First of all, I'd like to apologize for the lack of both the spring and summer issues of *Glen's Homophobia Newsletter*. I understand that you subscribed with the promise that this was to be a quarterly publication — four seasons' worth of news from the front lines of our constant battle against oppression. That was my plan. It's just that last spring and summer were so overwhelming that I, Glen, just couldn't deal with it all.

I'm hoping you'll understand. Please accept as consolation the fact that this issue is almost twice as long as the others. Keep in mind the fact that it's not easy to work forty hours a week *and* produce a quarterly publication. Also, while I'm at it, I'd like to mention that it would be wonderful if everyone who *read Glen's Homophobia Newsletter* also *subscribed* to *Glen's Homophobia Newsletter.* It seems that many of you are very generous when it comes to lending issues to your friends and family. That is all well and good as everyone should understand the passion with which we as a people are hated beyond belief. But at the same time, it *costs* to put out a newsletter and every dollar helps. It costs to gather data, to Xerox, to staple and mail, let alone the cost of my personal time and energies. So if you don't mind, I'd rather you mention *Glen's Homophobia Newsletter* to everyone you know but tell them they'll have to subscribe for themselves if they want the whole story. Thank you for understanding.

As I stated before, last spring and summer were very difficult for me. In late April Steve Dolger and I broke up and went our separate ways. Steve Dolger (see newsletters volume 2, nos. 1–4 and volume 3, no. 1) turned out to be the most *homophobic* homosexual I've ever had the displeasure of knowing. He lives in constant fear; afraid to make any kind of mature emotional commitment, afraid of growing old and losing what's left of his hair, and afraid to file his state and federal income taxes (which he has not done since 1987). Someday, perhaps someday very soon, Steve Dolger's past will come back to haunt him. We'll see how Steve and his little seventeen-year-old boyfriend feel when it happens!

Steve was very devious and cold during our breakup. I felt the chill of him well through the spring and late months of summer. With deep feelings come deep consequences and I, Glen, spent the last two seasons of my life in what I can only describe as a waking coma — blind to the world around me, deaf to the cries of suffering others, mutely unable to express the stirrings of my wildly shifting emotions.

I just came out of it last Thursday.

What has Glen discovered? I have discovered that living blind to the world around you has its drawbacks but, strangely, it also has its rewards. While I was cut off from the joys of, say, good food and laughter, I was also blind to the overwhelming *homophobia* that is our everlasting cross to bear.

I thought that for this edition of the newsletter I might write something along the lines of a *homophobia* Week in Review but this single week has been much too much for me. Rather, I will recount a single day.

My day of victimization began at 7:15 A.M. when I held the telephone receiver to my ear and heard Drew Pierson's voice shouting, "Fag, Fag, Fag," over and over and over again. It rings in my ears still. "Fag! I'll kick your ass good and hard the next time I see you. Goddamn you, Fag!" You, reader, are probably asking yourself, "Who is this Drew Pierson and why is he being so *homophobic* toward Glen?"

It all began last Thursday. I stopped into Dave's Kwik Stop on my way home from work and couldn't help but notice the cashier, a bulky, shorthaired boy who had "athletic scholarship" written all over his broad, dullish face and "Drew Pierson: I'm here to help!" written on a name tag pinned to his massive chest. I took a handbasket and bought, I believe, a bag of charcoal briquettes and a quartered fryer. At the register this Drew fellow rang up the items and said, "I'll bet you're going home to grill you some chicken."

I admitted that it was indeed my plan. Drew struck me as being very perceptive and friendly. Most of the Kwik Stop employees are *homophobic* but something about Drew's manner led me to believe that he was different, sensitive and open. That evening, sitting on my patio and staring into the glowing embers nestled in my tiny grill, I thought of Drew Pierson and for the first time in months I felt something akin to a beacon of hope flashing through the darkness of my mind. I, Glen, smiled.

I returned to Dave's Kwik Stop the next evening and bought some luncheon meat, a loaf of bread, potato chips, and a roll of toilet paper.

At the cash register Drew rang up my items and said, "I'll bet you're going on a picnic in the woods!"

The next evening I had plans to eat dinner at the condominium of my sister and her *homophobic* husband, Vince Covington (see newsletter volume 1, no. 1). On the way to their home I stopped at the Kwik Stop, where I bought a can of snuff. I don't use snuff, wouldn't think of it. I only ordered snuff because it was one of the few items behind the counter and on a lower shelf. Drew, as an employee, is forced to wear an awkward garment — sort of a cross between a vest and a sandwich board. The terrible, synthetic thing ties at the sides and falls practically to the middle of his thigh. I only ordered the snuff so that, as he bent over to fetch it, I might get a more enlightened view of Drew's physique. Regular readers of this newsletter will understand what I am talking about. Drew bent over and squatted on his heels, saying, "Which one? Tuberose? I used to like me some snuff. I'll bet you're going home to relax with some snuff, aren't you?"

The next evening, when I returned for more snuff, Drew explained that he was a freshman student at Carteret County Community College, where he majors in psychology. I was touched by his naïveté. CCCC might as well print their diplomas on tar paper. One might take a course in diesel mechanics or pipe fitting but under no circumstances should one study psychology at CCCC. That is where certified universities recruit their studies for *abnormal* psychology. CCCC is where the missing links brood and stumble and swing from the outer branches of our educational system.

Drew, bent over, said that he was currently taking a course in dreams. The teacher demands that each student keep a dream notebook, but Drew, exhausted after work, sleeps, he said, "like a gin-soaked log," and wakes remembering nothing.

I told him I've had some interesting dreams lately, because it's true, I have.

Drew said, "Symbolic dreams? Dreams that you could turn around when you're awake and make sense of?"

I said, yes, haunting dreams, meaningful, dense.

He asked then, hunkered down before the snuff, if I would relate my dreams to him. I answered, yes indeed, and he slapped a tin of snuff on the counter and said, "On the house!"

I returned home, my heart a bright balloon. Drew might be young, certainly — perhaps no older than, say, Steve Dolger's current boyfriend. He may not be able to hold his own during strenuous intellectual debate, but neither can most people. My buoyant spirit carried me home, where it was immediately deflated by the painful reminder that my evening meal was to consist of an ethnic lasagna pathetically submitted earlier that day by Melinda Delvecchio, a lingering temp haunting the secretarial pool over at the office in which I work. Melinda, stout, inquisitive, and bearded as a pot-bellied pig, has taken quite a shine to me. She is clearly and mistakenly in love with me and presents me, several times a week, with hideous dishes protected with foil. "Someone needs to fatten you up," she says, placing her eager hooves against my stomach. One would think that Melinda Delvecchio's kindness might come as a relief to the grinding *homophobia* I encounter at the office.

One might think that Melinda Delvecchio is thoughtful and generous until they pull back the gleaming foil under which lies her hateful concoction of overcooked pasta stuffed with the synthetic downy fluff used to fill plush toys and cheap cushions. Melinda Delvecchio is no friend of mind — far from it — and, regarding the heated "lasagna" steaming before me, I made a mental note to have her fired as soon as possible.

That night I dreamt that I was forced to leave my home and move underground into a dark, subterranean chamber with low, muddy ceilings and no furniture. That was bad enough, but to make matters worse I did not live alone but had to share the place with a community of honest-to-God trolls. These were small trolls with full beards and pointy, curled shoes. The trolls were hideously and relentlessly merry. They called me by name, saying, "Glen, so glad you could join us! Look, everybody, Glen's here! Welcome aboard, friend!" They were all so agreeable and satisfied with my company that I woke up sweating at 6:00 A.M. and could not return to sleep for fear of them.

I showered twice and shaved my face, passing the time until seven, at which time I phoned Drew at his parents' home. He answered groggy and confused. I identified myself and paused while he went to fetch a pencil and tablet with which to record my story.

Regular readers of *Glen's Homophobia Newsletter* know that I, Glen, honor truth and hold it above all other things. The truth, be it ugly or naked, does not frighten me. The meaner the truth, the harder I, Glen, stare it down. However, on this occasion I decided to make an exception. My dreaming of trolls means absolutely nothing. It's something that came to me in my sleep and is of no real importance. It is our waking dreams, our daydreams that are illuminating. Regular readers of *Glen's Homophobia Newsletter* know that I dream of the day when our people can walk the face of this earth free of the terrible *homophobia* that binds us. What are sleeping dreams but so much garbage? I can't bear to hear other people's dreams unless I myself am in them.

I put all these ideas together in a manageable sort of way and told Drew Pierson that I dreamt I was walking through a forest of angry, vindictive trees.

"Like those hateful trees in *The Wizard of Oz?*" he said. "Those mean trees that threw the apples?"

"Yes," I said, "exactly."

"Did any of them hit you?" he asked, concerned.

"A few."

"Ouch! Then what?"

I told him I came upon a clearing where I saw a single tree, younger than the rest but stocky, a husky, good-looking tree that spoke to me, saying, "I'll bet you're tired of being hated, aren't you?"

I could hear Drew scratching away with his pencil and repeating my dictation: "I . . . bet . . . you're . . . tired . . . of . . . being . . . hated . . ."

I told Drew that the tree had spoken in a voice exactly like his own, low and firm, yet open and friendly.

"Like my voice, really?" He seemed pleased. "Damn, my voice on a tree. I never thought about a thing like that."

That night I dreamt I was nailed to a cross that was decorated here and there with fragrant tulips. I glanced over at the cross next to me, expecting to see Christ, but instead, nailed there, I saw Don Rickles. We waved to each other and he mouthed the words, "Hang in there."

I called Drew the next morning and told him I once again dreamt I was in a forest clearing. Once again I found myself face-to-face with a husky tree.

Drew asked, "What did the tree say this time?"

I told him the tree said, "Let me out! Let me out! I'm yearning to break free."

"Break free of what?" he asked.

"Chains and limitations," I said. The tree said, "Strip me of my bark, strip me of my bark."

"The tree said that to you personally or was there someone else standing around?"

I told him the tree spoke to me personally and that I had no choice but to do as I was told. I peeled away the bark with my bare hands and out stepped Drew, naked and unashamed.

"Naked in the woods? I was in the woods naked like that? Then what?"

I told Drew I couldn't quite remember what happened next; it was right on the tip of my mind where I couldn't quite grasp it.

Drew said, "I want to know what I was doing naked in the woods is what I want to know."

I said, "Are you naked now?"

"Now?" Drew, apparently uncertain, took a moment before saying, "No. I got my underwear on."

I suggested that if he put the telephone receiver into the pouch of his briefs it might trigger something that would help me recall the rest of my dream.

I heard the phone muffle. When I yelled, "Did you put the phone where I told you to?" I heard a tiny, far-off voice say, "Yes, I sure did. It's there now."

"Jump up and down," I yelled. "Jump."

I heard shifting sounds as Drew's end of the telephone

jounced around in his briefs. I heard him yell, "Are you remembering yet?" And then, in the distance, I heard a woman's voice screaming, "Drew Pierson, what in the name of God are you doing with that telephone? Other people have to put their mouth on that thing too, you know. You should be strung up for doing a thing like that, Goddamn you." I heard Drew say that he was doing it in order to help someone remember a dream. Then I heard the words "moron," "shit for brains," and the inevitable "fag." As in "Some fag put you up to this, didn't he? Goddamn you."

Then Drew must have taken the receiver out of his briefs because suddenly I could hear him loud and clear and what I heard was *homophobia* at its worst. "Fag! Fag! I'll kick your ass good and hard the next time I see you. Goddamn you to hell." The words still echo in my mind.

I urge all my readers to BOYCOTT DAVE'S KWIK STOP. I urge you to phone Drew Pierson anytime day or night and tell him you dreamt you were sitting on his face. Drew Pierson's home (ophobic) telephone number is 787-5008. Call him and raise your voice against *homophobia!*

So that, in a nutshell, was my morning. I pulled myself together and subjected myself to the daily *homophobia* convention that passes as my job. Once there, I was scolded by my devious and *homophobic* department head for accidentally shredding some sort of disputed contract. Later that afternoon I was confronted, once again, by that casserole-wielding mastadon, Melinda Delvecchio, who grew tearful when informed that I would sooner dine on carpet remnants than another of her foil-covered ethnic slurs.

On my way home from the office I made the mistake of stopping at the Food Carnival, where I had no choice but to park in one of the so-called "handicapped" spaces. Once inside the store I had a tiff with the *homophobic* butcher over the dictionary definition of the word *cutlet*. I was completely ignored by the *homophobic* chimpanzee they've hired to run the produce department and I don't even want to talk about the cashier. After collecting my groceries I returned to the parking lot, where I encountered a *homophobe* in a wheelchair, relentlessly bashing my car again and again with the foot pedals of his little chariot. Regular readers of *Glen's Homophobia Newsletter* know that I, Glen, am not a violent man. Far from it. But in this case I had no choice but to make an exception. My daily *homophobia* quota had been exceeded and I, Glen, struck back with brute physical force.

Did it look good? No, it did not.

But I urge you, reader, to understand. Understand my position as it is your own.

Understand and subscribe, subscribe.

DON'S STORY

THANK you very, very much. I really just don't believe this is happening. I mean, this is what, the third time I've been up here tonight: Best Actor, Best Director, and now Best Picture. How am I going to carry all these awards home? In a truck? Ha ha.

Let me take a moment here because, like I said, I really didn't think this was going to happen. I've spent a great deal of time *wishing* it would happen but to have it actually take place is, ha ha, just a little overwhelming.

As I mentioned earlier this evening, while receiving my Academy Award for best actor, I arrived here in Los Angeles, California, almost a year ago with no experience whatsoever. I'd never acted or directed or produced a thing in my life. I was just a guy from Cumberland County, North Carolina — a man with a dream.

"What's going on here?" you're probably asking yourselves.

"Here this Don, this dreamer, never acted a day in his life and yet there he is sweeping the Academy Awards. How did he do it? What's so special about him?"

Well, that's what my movie, *Don's Story,* is all about. It's all right there: from my dropping out of high school at age seventeen to my packing for Hollywood at age thirty-six. I imagine it's what's *not* in the movie that probably interests you right now.

"How did he do it? This nobody, this dreamer."

Well, like I said, I left Cumberland almost a year ago on a Greyhound bus with a small bag of potato chips, eight dollars, and a dream. I stretched out and took two seats until somewhere outside Gatlinburg, when I was forced to surrender one of them to a woman by the name of Mrs. Patricia Toni. Mrs. Toni was headed to Encino, California.

"What's in Encino?" I asked, trying to be a good neighbor.

It turned out that Mrs. Toni's daughter was in Encino, in a hospital suffering from exhaustion. I don't know much about exhaustion, but I imagine it must be very tiring, so I said, "Oh, that's terrible." And she unfolded her newspaper and said, "You're darn right it's terrible."

At every stop along the way Mrs. Toni would buy the local newspaper and discuss the stories about crime and murder.

"Listen here where it says this man walked into a gas station and shot four people. Didn't even get gas or rob the place — just opened fire and killed four people. That's a low deed in my opinion. I think that's really terrible. If I was on that jury I'd convict him so fast it would make his head spin. I wouldn't waste time eating up the taxpayers' money. I'd just fire up the gas chamber and move on to the next case. The son of a bitch. It says here where he shot a five-year-old boy right through the neck. Bullet went in one side and out the other. I think that's terrible, don't you?"

Well, I didn't know the gunman. For all I know he might have had a pretty good reason to do what he did, but to make things easier I agreed and said I thought it was terrible.

"You're darn right it's terrible. Right through the neck. The neck is a very sensitive area. Everyone knows that. This is just terrible. I thought it was terrible the other day when that crackpot in Little Rock stabbed his mother's collie to death. Stabbed it seventeen times, a beautiful collie named Moxie. The mother cried and cried. Seventeen times he stabbed that dog. Once or twice would have done the job, but he did it seventeen times and I think that's terrible. Don't you?"

Crimes happen all across this country and Mrs. Toni made note of them day and night all the way to Reno, where she slept through our stop and missed her opportunity to buy a fresh newspaper. At this point, after having spent almost three days together, she finally asked me my name and where I was going and why, and I told her that my name was Don and that I was going to the Los Angeles area to make a name for myself in the motion picture industry, and she looked at me and said, "You've *got* to be kidding — *You?*" Then she turned to the man across the aisle and pointed at me and said, "This one thinks he's going to be some kind of a movie star." And she put her hands on her stomach and bent over laughing and I just sort of . . . punched her. I jabbed her real quick with the bathroom key I'd gotten at the last station. I just sort of . . . poked her with it just real . . . quick and, ha ha, she made just the biggest stink about it. She made the bus driver pull over and she lifted her sweater and showed everybody the little mark on her side — just a little nick, and she was pointing at me and saying, "I think this is terrible. I mean it. Here I get on this bus to visit my daughter who is clinically exhausted and I'm practically stabbed to death in broad daylight. This is the sort of thing that makes the papers as far as I'm concerned. 'Woman Stabbed on Bus.' This is terrible."

So the bus driver threw me off onto the dusty highway. No refund or anything, just tossed me out. By this time I had only two dollars left so I stuck out my thumb and was picked up by a man named Enrique Moldonato and tonight, standing onstage here at the Academy Awards, I would like to thank him publicly. As luck would have it he was going all the way to Los Angeles and dropped me off at a Laundromat close to his home. Luckily, the Laundromat had a phone book and I had a quarter so I put two and two together and phoned Paramount Pictures. When the receptionist answered I said, "Let me speak to the person in charge there."

She said, "One moment, please."

Then, in the background I heard her say, "Mr. Tartikoff, you have a phone call."

And I heard him say, "Oh, good."

He came to the phone and I said, "Mr. Tartikoff, my name is Don Singleton and I'd like to make a motion picture."

He said, "Hmmmm. A motion picture about what?"

And I looked over and saw someone empty the lint tray from one of the dryers and I said, "A motion picture about my life."

"I'm all ears, Don," Mr. Tartikoff said.

Just then the operator came on the line and told me to deposit more coins and Mr. Tartikoff said, "Don, are you calling from a pay phone?"

I confessed that I was and he asked if there was some way we might talk in person, so I gave him the address and shortly thereafter a big limo pulled up and Mr. Tartikoff entered and put his hands to his mouth and yelled, "Is there a Don Singleton here?" and I said, "Yes, that's me."

We shook hands and he looked around and he said, "Say, Don, this place is really damp. What do you say we go someplace else?"

He said he'd been invited to a big celebrity party and asked would I like to come along and I thought about it for about, ha ha, two seconds and said sure. Then his driver opened the door and we got into the limousine and on the way to the party Mr. Tartikoff, Brandon, asked me questions about my life.

He poured us each a glass of scotch from the bar and studied me and said, "What are you, Don — about thirty-five years old?"

"Thirty-six."

"Have you ever worked?"

I told him I'd worked almost four years as a dishwasher at the K&W Cafeteria. I worked there from the age of seventeen until I was twenty-one, when I got fired for spitting in the food.

"They fired you for *that*?" Brandon said. "That's crazy. Why, everyone I know spits in things all the time." He spit into his glass and drank it. "That's no reason to *fire* anyone for God's sake."

Then I spit on my fingers and leaned over and rubbed it into the driver's neck.

Brandon looked at me then and said, "I've got a feeling about you, Don — a good one," and we chinked our glasses in a toast.

At about this time, the limousine turned off the road and we headed up a long tree-lined driveway, up to a big mansion with white columns and stained-glass windows and a shallow moat filled with swans and turtles and someone came and opened the limo door and I looked up and saw Barbra Streisand and she was wearing . . . well, the exact same thing she's wearing tonight as a matter of fact. She and Brandon embraced and then she turned to me and raised her eyebrows like, "Who the heck is this?" Brandon told Barbra Streisand that my name was Don and that I used to wash dishes at K&W Cafeteria and, ha ha, I tell you, Barbra Streisand just couldn't ask enough questions.

"A dishwasher! Tell me, was it a conveyor run-through Waste King Jet System or a double hot sink layout? What detergents did you use? At what temperature does a drinking glass become quote unquote 'clean'?" She took my arm and led me into the house, which was just absolutely teeming with celebrities: Joey Bishop, Faye Dunaway, Shari Lewis, Kevin Costner, Gene Rayburn, Tatum O'Neal, Tom Cruise, Cathy Lee Crosby, Carol Channing, Buddy Ebsen — the list goes on and on and on. Barbra Streisand handed me a champagne cocktail and introduced me around and, ha ha, I felt like giving a press conference, so many people asking questions about my life.

"What did you do after you lost your job at the cafeteria?" Chastity Bono asked.

And I said, "Nothing, just sort of hung around the house."

Michael Douglas asked what my parents had to say about *that,* and I said, "Well, you know my parents." And then I realized that no, these celebrities *didn't* know my parents. In my movie, *Don's Story,* my parents are played by Charles Bronson and Don Rickles. I think they both did a fantastic job — especially Don Rickles, who played the part of my mother. Quite a few actresses were eager for that role, but as director I chose Don Rickles not because my mother is funny — far from it — and not to boost Mr. Rickles's career, but because, ha ha, you put a wig on that guy and he looks just exactly like her. Ha ha. And Charles Bronson — what can I say? He's one of the best in the business. And that's the funny thing about show business, that it's a constant learning experience . . . for everybody. Last year when those celebrities asked what my parents were like, I had a hard time coming up with the words.

I lost my job at the K&W at the age of twenty-one and for the next fourteen years my parents never, for one moment, let up on me. They were all the time trying to make me feel bad for being myself and not working. If I had a nickel for every time they pounded on my bedroom door screaming, "WHAT ARE YOU DOING IN THERE?" I'd have several million dollars. Well, ha ha, I guess now I *do* have several million dollars but I would have had it a lot sooner.

"WHAT ARE YOU DOING IN THERE?"

And I'd say that I was planning to take Hollywood by storm and they'd yell, "YOU'RE OUT OF YOUR MIND. YOU'RE INSANE. DO YOU UNDERSTAND? INSANE. COME OUT OF THAT ROOM AND GET A JOB. YOUR BROTHER HAS A JOB AND HE'S MISSING HIS LEFT HAND — IF HE CAN WORK SO CAN YOU. DO YOU HEAR ME? COME OUT OF THAT BEDROOM."

"That must have been very difficult for you," Dr. Joyce Brothers said. And I admitted that, yes, it was. Then someone asked what kind of a lock I had on my bedroom door and Brandon Tartikoff caught my eye and made a cutting gesture against his throat and, ha ha, even though I'd been in Hollywood for less than two hours I knew what *that* meant, which probably has a lot to do with why I've walked away with tonight's Best Director award. "Cut!" Thanks, Brandon.

I hated saying good-bye to all of my wonderful new show business friends but it was time to go so Brandon led me out the door to our waiting limo. And just as I was settling into the backseat I saw Barbra Streisand turn to Vincent Price and say, "I like that kid. He's a survivor."

So are you, Barbra. So are you.

We left the party and went to a restaurant named Spago, where Brandon and I spent the next several hours talking and eating spaghetti. He seemed so interested in every aspect of my life and was full of questions.

"So tell me, Don, after you left the cafeteria you mean to say you did absolutely *nothing* for the next fourteen years? God, that's fascinating."

I noticed people at the surrounding tables perk up and try to listen in on our conversation so Brandon had us moved to a private booth.

"What was your day like? When would you wake up?"

I told him I'd usually open my eyes at around one-thirty or two but wouldn't get out of bed until two forty-five, when my mother put on her fluorescent vest and left the house to do volunteer crosswalk service at Brooks Elementary. Then I'd go downstairs and root around the kitchen and watch TV until around four o'clock, when her car would pull up in the driveway, at which point I'd go back to my room and lock the door and stare at my hands until around five-thirty.

"I noticed your hands," Brandon said. "They're really special. When was the last time you trimmed your fingernails?"

"Nineteen eighty-three, eighty-four."

"Do you ever *wash* your hands?" he asked.

"Maybe," I said. "Maybe not." I wasn't being difficult — just mysterious.

Just then the waiter delivered our check and he said, "I

noticed your hands the moment you walked in. They're fascinating. Hands tell so much about a person. I think you should get a job here!"

"Back off," Brandon said. "I think Don's had enough restaurant work to last him the rest of his life."

When we got back to the limo Brandon asked if I had a place to stay and when I confessed that I did not he used his car phone and made a reservation at the Beverly Wilshire hotel. Then he said, "So, all right, Don, say it's five-thirty and you've spent the late afternoon looking at your hands. Then what?"

I told him that then my father would come home from work and, ha ha, Oh, Lord, I could hear him all the way upstairs. "WHERE IS HE? WHAT'S HE DONE TODAY? WHAT DO YOU MEAN YOU HAVEN'T SEEN HIM?" Then he'd look in the refrigerator and start yelling, "GODDAMN HIM. WHERE THE HELL IS THAT LEFTOVER STUFFING FROM LAST NIGHT? GODDAMN IT. HEY YOU UP THERE — I'M TALKING TO YOU."

"That's a very funny impersonation," Brandon said. "I mean, I don't know the man from Adam, but I can picture him perfectly. Do more, please."

"WHAT THE HELL IS YOUR PROBLEM? HERE I'VE GOT A FULL-GROWN SON WHO WON'T FIND A JOB — WON'T EVEN LEAVE THE GODDAMNED HOUSE AND COMES DOWN HERE WHEN MY BACK IS TURNED AND EATS MY STUFFING. I WORKED HARD FOR THAT STUFFING. DO YOU HEAR ME? FROM NOW ON THIS KITCHEN IS OFF-LIMITS TO YOU, MISTER. NO MORE FOOD FOR YOU. YOU'LL BE EATING THE INSULATION OUT OF YOUR WALLS BY THE TIME I'M FINISHED WITH YOU, GODDAMN YOU."

Then he'd come pounding on my door and I'd put on my headphones and listen to records in order to drown him out.

"Did you have a big music library?" Brandon asked.

I told him that I had two records, Uriah Heap's "Look at

Yourself" and "Don't Look Down" by The Ozark Mountain Daredevils — both records I had bought while working at the cafeteria.

"Those are really great records," Brandon said. We arrived at the hotel and checked in to the room, which was, ha ha, really big, with a living room and a bedroom and curtains and a coffee table. I just couldn't get over it. Brandon went over to the bar and poured us a nightcap and said, "All right, Don, so you listen to your records — then what?"

I explained that I'd listen to the records until after my parents fell asleep, usually around eleven-thirty or twelve, and then I'd go downstairs and see what I could find for supper. After about 1986 my parents would just cook enough food for the two of them, but I could always find a little something. Sometimes it might be just a couple handfuls of raw macaroni or a half-stick of butter, but it was always something. Then I'd root around for change in my mother's purse or under the sofa cushions.

"Every night?"

"Every night, and over the years it really, ha ha, added up. Then I'd watch TV until the regular programming went off the air and the pattern shows came on. I'd watch maybe a few hours of the pattern to clear my mind and then I'd go to bed and start all over again the next day."

Brandon offered me a lit cigarette and looked down at his nightcap, asking, "Why did you leave, Don? Why?"

I told him I left the day after my father put padlocks on the refrigerator and all the kitchen cabinets. At that point I counted my change, scratched and ripped up every piece of furniture in the house, and walked out the door to meet my destiny.

Brandon shook his head and said, "Don, this story has *everything*."

And I signed a contract that very night. It was just that simple — just the way I always thought it would be.

And I'd like to thank Brandon for recognizing my abilities and giving me complete artistic control from casting right on up. I'd like to thank Uriah Heap and The Ozark Mountain

Daredevils for providing the musical score. I'd like to thank all the members of the academy for their votes but, most of all, I'd like to thank the citizens of this country for making *Don's Story* the number-one top box office draw that it is because, let me tell you, academy or no academy, it is your continuing support, loyalty, and devotion that make this award so heavy and meaningful. Certain people might be watching this broadcast with rage and jealousy — certain people who have mistreated and underestimated me are probably wishing they had the chance to take it all back and start over again with a fresh slate but I'm afraid it's too late for that. It's something I wouldn't mind talking about but I see our host off to the side of the stage pointing to his watch and so I'll take that as a hint and say good night, thank you, I love you.

SEASON'S GREETINGS TO OUR FRIENDS AND FAMILY!!!

**M**ANY of you, our friends and family, are probably taken aback by this, our annual holiday newsletter. You've read of our recent tragedy in the newspapers and were no doubt thinking that, what with all of their sudden legal woes and "hassles," the Dunbar clan might just stick their heads in the sand and avoid this upcoming holiday season altogether!!

You're saying, "There's no way the Dunbar family can grieve their terrible loss *and* carry on the traditions of the season. No family is *that* strong," you're thinking to yourselves.

Well, think again!!!!!!!!!!!!

While this past year has certainly dealt our family a heavy hand of sorrow and tribulation, we have (so far!) weathered the storm and shall continue to do so! Our tree is standing tall in the living room, the stockings are hung, and we are eagerly awaiting the arrival of a certain portly gentleman who goes by the name "Saint Nick"!!!!!!!!!!!!

Our trusty PC printed out our wish lists weeks ago and now we're cranking it up again to wish you and yours The Merriest of Christmas Seasons from the entire Dunbar family: Clifford, Jocelyn, Kevin, Jacki, Kyle, and Khe Sahn!!!!!

Some of you are probably reading this and scratching your heads over the name "Khe Sahn." "That certainly doesn't fit with the rest of the family names," you're saying to yourself. "What, did those crazy Dunbars get themselves a Siamese cat?"

You're close.

To those of you who live in a cave and haven't heard the news, allow us to introduce Khe Sahn Dunbar who, at the age of twenty-two, happens to be the newest member of our family.

Surprised?

JOIN THE CLUB!!!!!!!

It appears that Clifford, husband of yours truly and father to our three natural children, accidentally planted the seeds for Khe Sahn twenty-two years ago during his stint in . . . where else?

VIETNAM!!!!

This was, of course, years before Clifford and I were married. At the time of his enlistment we were pre-engaged and the long period of separation took its toll on both of us. I corresponded regularly. (I wrote him every single day, even when I couldn't think of anything interesting. His letters were much less frequent but I saved all four of them!)

While I had both the time and inclination to put my feelings into envelopes, Clifford, along with thousands of other American soldiers, had no such luxury. While the rest of us were watching the evening news in our safe and comfortable homes, he was *making* the evening news, standing waist high in a stagnant foxhole. The hazards and the torments of war are something that, luckily, most of us cannot begin to imagine and, for that, we should all count our blessings.

Clifford Dunbar, twenty-two years ago, a young man in a war-torn country, made a mistake. A terrible, heinous mistake. A stupid, thoughtless, permanent mistake with dreadful, haunting consequences.

But who are you, who are any of us, to judge him for it? Especially now, with Christmas at our heels. Who are we to judge?

When his tour of duty ended Clifford returned home, where, after making the second biggest mistake of his life (I am referring to his brief eight-month "marriage" to Doll Babcock), he and I were reunited. We lived, you might remember, in that tiny apartment over on Halsey Street. Clifford had just begun his satisfying career at Sampson Interlock and I was working part-time, accounting for Hershel Beck when . . . along came the children!!!!!! We struggled and saved and eventually (finally!!) bought our house on Tiffany Circle, number 714, where the Dunbar clan remains nested to this very day!!!!

It was here, 714 Tiffany Circle, where I first encountered Khe Sahn, who arrived at our door on (as fate would have it) Halloween!!!

I recall mistaking her for a Trick-or-Treater! She wore, I remember, a skirt the size of a beer cozy, a short, furry jacket, and, on her face, enough rouge, eye shadow, and lipstick to paint our entire house, inside and out. She's a very small person and I mistook her for a child, a child masquerading as a prostitute. I handed her a fistful of chocolate nougats, hoping that, like the other children, she would quickly move on to the next house.

But Khe Sahn was no Trick-or-Treater.

I started to close the door but was interrupted by her interpreter, a very feminine-looking man carrying an attaché case. He introduced himself in English and then turned to Khe Sahn, speaking a language I have sadly come to recognize as Vietnamese. While our language flows from our mouths, the Vietnamese language sounds as though it is being forced from the speaker by series of heavy and merciless blows to the stomach. The words themselves are the sounds of pain. Khe Sahn responded to the interpreter, her voice as high-pitched and relentless as a car alarm. The two of them stood on my doorstep, screeching away in Vietnamese while I stood by, frightened and confused.

I am still, to this day, frightened and confused. Very much so. It is frightening that, after all this time, a full-grown bastard (I use that word technically) can cross the seas and make herself comfortable in my home, all with the blessing of our government. Twenty-two years ago Uncle Sam couldn't stand the Vietnamese. Now he's dressing them like prostitutes and moving them into our houses!!!! Out of nowhere this young woman has entered our lives with the force and mystery of the Swine Flu and there appears to be nothing we can do about it. Out of nowhere this land mine knocks upon our door and we are expected to recognize her as our child!!!!????????

Clifford likes to say that the Dunbar children inherited their mother's looks and their father's brains. It's true: Kevin, Jackelyn, and Kyle are all just as good-looking as they can possibly be! And smart? Well, they're smart enough, smart like their father, with the exception of our oldest son, Kevin. After graduating Moody High with honors, Kevin is currently enrolled in his third year at Feeny State, majoring in chemical engineering. He's made the honor roll every semester and there seems to be no stopping him!!! A year and a half left to go and already the job offers are pouring in!

We love you, Kevin!!!!!!!!!!!!!!!!!!!

We sometimes like to joke that when God handed out brains to the Dunbar kids He saw Kevin standing first in line and awarded him the whole sack!!! What the other children lack in brains they seem to make up for in one way or another. They have qualities and personalities and make observations, unlike Khe Sahn, who seems to believe she can coast through life on her looks alone!! She hasn't got the ambition God gave a sparrow! She arrived in this house six weeks ago speaking only the words "Daddy," "Shiny," and "Five dollar now."

Quite a vocabulary!!!!!!!!!!

While an industrious person might buckle down and seriously study the language of her newly adopted country, Khe Sahn appeared to be in no hurry whatsoever. When asked a simple question such as, "Why don't you go back where you came from?" she would touch my hand and launch into a spasm of Vietnamese drivel — as if I were the outsider, expected to learn *her* language! We were visited several times by Lonnie Tipit, that "interpreter," that "man" who accompanied Khe Sahn on her first visit. Mr. Tipit seemed to feel that the Dunbar door was open for him anytime, day or night. He'd drop by (most often during the supper hours) and, between helpings of *my* home-cooked meals (thank you very much), "touch base" with his "friend," Khe Sahn. "I don't think she's getting enough exposure to the community," he would say. "Why don't you start taking her around town, to church get-togethers and local events?" Well, that was easy for *him* to say! I told him, I said, "*You* try taking a girl in a halter top to a confirmation class. *You* take her to the Autumn Craft Caravan and watch her snatch every shiny object that catches her eye. I've learned my lesson already." Then he and Khe Sahn would confer in Vietnamese and he would listen, his eyes fixed upon me as if I were a witch he had once read about in books but did not recognize without a smoldering kettle and a broom. Oh, I knew that look!

Lonnie Tipit went so far as to suggest that we hire him as Khe Sahn's English tutor at, get this, seventeen dollars an hour!!!!!!!!!! Seventeen dollars an hour so she can learn to lisp and twitter and flutter her hands like two small birds? NO, THANK YOU!!!!!!! Oh, I saw right through Lonnie Tipit. While he pretended to care for Khe Sahn I understood that his true interest was in my son Kyle. "How's the schoolwork coming, Kyle? Working hard or hardly working?" and "Say, Kyle, what do you think about this new sister of yours? Is she the greatest or what?"

It wasn't difficult to see through Lonnie Tipit. He wanted one thing and one thing only. "If not me, then I can suggest another tutor," he said. Someone like who? Someone like him?

Regardless of who the English teacher was, I am not in the habit of throwing my money away. And that, my friends, is what it would have amounted to. Why not hire an expensive private tutor to teach the squirrels to speak in French! It would be no more ridiculous than teaching Khe Sahn English. A person has to *want* to learn. I know that. Apparently, back in Ho Chi Minh City, Her Majesty was treated like a queen and sees no reason to change her ways!!!! Her Highness rises at around noon, wolfs down a fish or two (all she eats is fish and chicken breasts), and settles herself before the makeup mirror, waiting for her father to return home from work. At the sound of his car in the drive-way she perks up and races to the door like a spaniel, panting and wagging her tail to beat the band! Suddenly she is eager to please and attempt conversation!! Well, I don't know how they behave in Vietnam, but in the United States it is not customary for a half-dressed daughter to offer her father a five-dollar massage!!! After having spent an exhausting day attempting to communicate a list of simple chores, I would stand in amazement at Khe Sahn's sudden grasp of English when faced with my husband.

"Daddy happy five dollar shiny now, OK?"

"You big feet friendly with ABC Khe Sahn. You Big Bird Daddy Grover."

Apparently she had picked up a few words while watching "Sesame Street."

"Daddy special special funky fresh jam party commercial free jam."

She began listening to the radio.

Khe Sahn treats our youngest son, Kyle, with complete indifference, which is probably a blessing in disguise. This entire episode has been very difficult for Kyle, who, at age fifteen, tends to be the artistic loner of the family. He keeps to himself, spending many hours in his bedroom, where he burns incense, listens to music, and carves gnomes out of soap. Kyle is very good-looking and talented and we are looking forward to the day when he sets aside his jackknife and bar of Irish Spring and begins "carving out" a future rather than a shriveled troll! He is at that very difficult age but we pray he will grow out of it and follow his brother's footsteps to success before it is too late. Hopefully, the disasters of his sister, Jackelyn, will open his eyes to the hazards of drugs, the calamity of a thoughtless, premature marriage, and the heartaches of parenthood!

We had, of course, warned our daughter against marrying Timothy Speaks. We warned, threatened, cautioned, advised, what have you — but it did no good as a young girl, with all the evidence before her, sees only what she *wants* to see. The marriage was bad enough but the news of her pregnancy struck her father and me with the force of a hurricane.

Timothy Speaks, the father of our grandchild? How could it be????

Timothy Speaks, who had so many pierced holes in his ears you could have torn the lobe right off, effortlessly ripped it loose the same way you might separate a stamp from a sheet.

Timothy Speaks, who had his back and neck tattooed with brilliant flames. His neck!!!

We told Jacki, "One of these days he's going to have to grow up and find a job, and when he does, those employers are going to wonder why he's wearing a turtleneck under his business suit. People with tattooed necks do not, as a rule, hold down high-paying jobs," we said.

She ran back to Timothy repeating our warning.... Lo and behold, two days later, *she* showed up with a tattooed neck as well!!!!! They even made plans to have their baby tattooed!!!! A tattoo, on an infant!!!!!!!!!!!

Timothy Speaks held our daughter in a web of madness that threatened to ensnare the entire Dunbar family. It was as if he held her under a perverse spell, convincing her, little by little, to destroy the lives of those around her.

The Jackelyn Dunbar-Speaks who lived with Timothy in that squalid "space" on West Vericose Avenue bore no resemblance to the beautiful girl pictured in our photo albums. The sensitive and considerate daughter we once knew became, under his fierce coaching, a mean-spirited, unreliable, and pregnant ghost who eventually gave birth to a ticking time bomb!!!!!

We, of course, saw it coming. The child, born September tenth under the influence of drugs, spent the first two months of his life in the critical care unit of St. Joe's Hospital. (At a whopping cost and guess who paid the bill for *that* one?) Faced with the concrete responsibility of fatherhood, Timothy Speaks abandoned his sick wife and child. Suddenly. Gone. Poof!

Surprised?

We saw it coming and are happy to report that, as of this writing, we have no idea where he is or what he is up to. (We could guess, but why bother?)

We have all read the studies and understand that a drug-addicted baby faces a difficult, uphill battle in terms of living a normal life. This child, having been given the legal name "Satan Speaks" would, we felt, have a harder time than most. We were lucky enough to get Jacki into a fine treatment center on the condition that the child remain here with us until which time (if ever) she is able to assume responsibility for him. The child arrived at our home on November tenth and shortly thereafter, following her initial withdrawal, Jacki granted us permission to address it as "Don." Don, a nice, simple name.

The name change enabled us to look upon the baby without having to consider the terrible specter of his father, Timothy Speaks. It made a difference, believe me.

While I could not describe him as being a "normal" baby, taking care of young Don gave me a great deal of pleasure. Terribly insistent, prone to hideous rashes, a twenty-four-hour round-the-clock screamer, he was our grandchild and we loved him. Knowing that he would physically grow to adulthood while maintaining the attention span of a common housefly did not, in the least bit, diminish our feelings for him.

Clifford would sometimes joke that Don was a "Crack Baby" because he woke us at the crack of dawn!

I would then take the opportunity to mention that Khe Sahn was something of a "Crack Baby" herself, wandering around our house all hours of the day and night wearing nothing but a pair of hot pants and a glorified sports bra. Most nights, the dinnertime napkin in her lap provided more coverage than she was accustomed to!!! Clifford suggested that I buy her a few decent dresses and a couple pairs of jeans and I tried, oh, how I tried! I sat with her, leafing through catalogs, and watched as she pawed the expensive designer outfits. I walked with her through Cut Throat's and Discount Plus and watched as she turned up her nose at their sensibly priced clothing. I don't know about you, but in *this* family the children are rewarded for hard work. Call me old-fashioned but if you want a fifty-dollar sweater you have to prove that you deserve it! If I've said it once I've said it a thousand times: "A family is not a charitable organization." Khe Sahn wanted something for nothing and I buttoned my purse and said the most difficult word a parent can say, "No!" I made her several outfits, sewed them with my own hands, two floor-length dresses, beautiful burlap dresses, but did she wear them? Of course not!!!

She continued in her usual fashion, trotting about the house in her underwear! When the winter winds began to blow she took to draping herself in a bed blanket, huddling beside the fireplace. While her "Poor Little Match Girl" routine might win a Tony Award on Broadway it did nothing for this ticket holder!

She carried on, following at Clifford's heels, until Thanksgiving Day, when she was introduced to our son Kevin, home for the holiday. One look at Kevin and it was "Clifford? Clifford who?" as far as Khe Sahn was concerned. One look at our handsome son and the "Shivering Victim" dropped her blanket and showed her true colors. It is a fact that she appeared at our Thanksgiving table wearing nothing but a string bikini!!!!!!!!!

"Not in *my* house," said yours truly! When I demanded she change into one of the dresses I had sewn for her, Khe Sahn frowned into her cranberry sauce, pretending not to understand. Clifford and Kevin tried to convince me that, in Vietnam, it is customary for the women to wear swimsuits on Thanksgiving

Day but I still don't believe a word of it. Since when do the Vietnamese observe Thanksgiving? What do those people have to be thankful for?

She ruined our holiday dinner with her giggling, coy games. She sat beside Kevin until, insisting she had seen a spider in her chair, she moved into his lap!! "You new funky master jam party mix silly fresh spider five dollar Big Bird."

Those of you who know Kevin understand that, while he is an absolute whip at some things, he is terribly naive at others. Tall and good-looking, easy with a smile and a kind word, Kevin has been the target of many a huntress. He is both smart and foolish: it is his gift and his weakness, bound together, constantly struggling for control. He has always had more than his fair share of opportunists, both at Moody High and Feeny State. Always the gentleman, he treated the young ladies like glass, which, looking back, was appropriate because you could see through each and every one of them. When he asked to bring a date home for Thanksgiving I said I thought it was a bad idea as we were all under more than enough stress already. Looking back, I wish he *had* brought a date, as it might have dampened the sky-high hopes and aspirations of Khe Sahn, his half-sister!!!!!!!!!!

"Me no big big potato spoon fork tomorrow? Kevin have big big shiny face like hand of chicken soon with funky crazy Sesame Street jammy jam."

I could barely choke down my meal and found myself counting the minutes before Kevin, the greatest joy of our lives, called an end to the private English lesson he gave Khe Sahn in her bedroom, got into his car, and returned to Feeny State.

As I mentioned before, Kevin has always been a very caring person, always going out of his way to lend a hand or comfort a stranger. Being as that is his nature, he returned to school and, evidently, began phoning Khe Sahn, sometimes speaking with the aid of a Vietnamese student who acted as an interpreter. He was, in his own way, foolishly trying to make her feel welcome and adjust to life in her new, highly advanced country. He even went out of his way to drive all the way home in order to take her out and introduce her to the ways of nightlife in this, her adopted land. That is the Kevin we all know and love, always trying to help a person less intelligent than himself, bending over backwards to coax a smile!

Unfortunately, Khe Sahn misinterpreted his interest as a declaration of romantic concern. She took to "manning" the telephone twenty-four hours a day, hovering above it and regarding it as though it were a living creature. Whenever (God forbid!) someone called for Clifford, Kyle, or me, she would simply hang up!!!!

How's *that* for an answering service!!!!!!!!!!!!!!

Eventually, recognizing that her behavior bordered on madness, I had a word with her.

"HE'S NOT FOR YOU," I yelled. (I have been criticized for yelling, told that it doesn't serve any real purpose when speaking to a foreigner, but at least it gets their attention!) "HE'S MY SON IN COLLEGE. MY SON ON THE DEAN'S LIST, NOT FOR YOU."

She was perched beside the telephone with a curling iron in her hand. At the sound of my voice she instinctively turned her attention elsewhere.

"BOTH MY SON AND MY HUSBAND ARE OFF-LIMITS AS FAR AS YOU'RE CONCERNED, DO YOU UNDERSTAND? THEY ARE EACH RELATED TO YOU IN ONE WAY OR ANOTHER AND THAT MAKES IT WRONG. AUTOMATICALLY WRONG. BAD, BAD, WRONG! WRONG AND BAD TOGETHER FOR THE KHE SAHN TO BE WITH JOCELYN'S SON OR HUSBAND. BAD AND WRONG. DO YOU UNDERSTAND WHAT I AM SAYING NOW?"

She looked up for a moment or two before returning her attention to the electrical cord.

I gave up. Trying to explain moral principles to Khe Sahn was like reviewing a standard 1040 tax form with a house cat! She understands only what she chooses to understand. Say the word "shopping" and, quicker than you can blink, she's sitting in the front seat of the car! Try a more complicated word such as "sweep" or "iron" and she shrugs her shoulders and retreats to the bedroom.

"VACUUM," I would say. "VACUUM THE CARPET."

In response she would jangle her bracelet or observe her fingernails.

In a desperate attempt to make myself understood I would pull out the vacuum cleaner and demonstrate.

"LOOK AT JOCELYN. JOCELYN VACUUMS THE CARPET. LA LA LA!! IT IS MUCH FUN TO VACUUM. IT IS AN ENJOYMENT AND A PLEASURE TO CLEAN MY HOME WITH A VACUUM. LA LA LA!!"

I tried to convey it as a rewarding exercise but, by the time I finally sparked her interest I was finished with the job.

As I said earlier, Khe Sahn understands only what she wants to understand. Looking back, I suppose I had no valid reason to trust her sudden willingness to lend a hand but, on the day in question, I was nearing the end of my rope.

We were approaching Christmas, December sixteenth, when I made the thoughtless mistake of asking her to watch the child while I ran some errands. With a needy, shriveled newborn baby, a teenaged son, and a twenty-two-year-old, half-dressed "stepdaughter" in my house, my hands were full from one moment to the next, twenty-eight hours a day!!!! It was nine days before Christmas and, busy as I was, I hadn't bought a single gift. (Santa, where are you????????)

On that early afternoon Kyle was in school, Clifford was at the office, and Khe Sahn was seated beside the telephone, picking at a leftover baked fish with her bare hands.

"WATCH THE BABY," I said. "WATCH DON, THE BABY, WHILE I GO OUT."

She considered her greasy fingers.

"YOU WATCH BABY DON WHILE JOCELYN GOES SHOPPING FOR SPECIAL PRESENT FOR THE KHE

SAHN!" I said. "HO, HO, HO, SPECIAL CHRISTMAS FOR THE KHE SAHN. HO, HO!"

At the mention of the word "shopping" she perked up and gave me her full attention. Having heard the radio and watched TV, she understood Christmas as an opportunity to receive gifts and was in the habit of poring over the mail-order catalogs and expressing her desires with the words "Ho, Ho, Ho."

I clearly remember my choice of words on that cold and cloudy December afternoon. I did not say "baby-sit," fearing that she might take me at my word and literally sit upon the baby.

"WATCH THE BABY," I said to that twenty-two-year-old adult on the afternoon of December sixteenth.

"WATCH THE BABY," I said as we climbed the stairs toward the bedroom that she and Don shared. Khe Sahn had been sleeping in Kevin's vacant bedroom until, following her Thanksgiving high jinks, I decided to move her into the nursery with Don.

"WATCH THE BABY," I repeated as we stood over the crib and observed the wailing infant. I picked him up and rocked him gently as he struggled in my arms. "WATCH BABY."

"Watch Baby," Khe Sahn responded, holding out her arms to accept him. "Watch Baby for Jocelyn get shop special HO, HO, HO, Khe Sahn fresh shiny."

"Exactly," I said, laying a hand on her shoulder.

How foolish I was to have honestly believed that she was finally catching on! I was, at that moment in time, convinced of her sincerity. I was big enough to set aside all of the trouble she had visited upon our household and give her another chance! "That is all behind us now," I said to myself, watching her cradle the wailing child.

Oh, what a fool I was!!!!!!!!!!!!!!

Leaving the house and driving toward White Paw Center I felt a sense of relief I had not known in quite a while. This was the first time in weeks I had allowed myself a moment alone and, with six Dunbar wish lists burning a hole in my pocket, I intended to make the most of it!!!

I can't account for every moment of my afternoon. Never did it occur to me that I would one day be called upon to do so but, that being the case, I will report what I remember. I can comfortably testify that, on the afternoon of December sixteenth, I visited the White Paw Shopping Center, where I spent a brief amount of time in The Slack Heap, searching for a gift for Kyle. I found what he wanted but not in his size. I then left The Slack Heap and walked over to ——— & ———, where I bought a ——— for my daughter Jacki. (I'm not going to ruin anyone's Christmas surprises here. Why should I?) I stuck my head inside Turtleneck Crossing and searched for candles at Wax and Wane. I bought a gift for Clifford at ———, and I suppose I browsed. There are close to a hundred shops at the White Paw Center and you'll have to forgive me if I can't provide a detailed list of how long I spent in this or that store. I shopped until I grew wary of the time. On the way home I stopped at The Food Carnival and bought a few items. It was getting dark, perhaps four-thirty, when I pulled into the driveway of our home on Tiffany Circle. I collected my packages from the car and entered my home, where I was immediately struck by the eerie silence. "This doesn't feel right to me," I remember saying to myself. It was an intuition, a mother's intuition, that unexplainable language of the senses. I laid down my bags and was startled by the sound they made — the crisp noise of paper bags settling against the floor. The problem was that I could hear the sound at all! Normally I would have heard nothing over the chronic bleating of Baby Don and the incessant blaring radio of Khe Sahn.

"Something is wrong," I said to myself. "Something is terribly, terribly wrong."

Before calling out for Khe Sahn or checking on the baby I instinctively phoned the police. I then stood there, stock-still in the living room, staring at my shopping bags until they arrived (twenty-seven minutes later!!).

At the sound of the squad car in the driveway, Khe Sahn made an entrance, parading down the stairs in a black lace half-slip and a choker made from the cuff of Kevin's old choir robe.

"WHERE IS THE BABY?" I asked her. "WHERE IS DON?"

Accompanied by the police we went upstairs into the nursery and stood beside the empty crib.

"WHERE IS MY GRANDCHILD, DON? WHAT HAVE YOU DONE TO THE BABY?"

Khe Sahn, of course, said nothing. It is part of her act to tug at her hemline and feign shyness when first confronted by strangers. We left her standing there while the police and I began our search. We combed the entire house, the officers and I, before finally finding the helpless baby in the laundry room, warm but lifeless in the dryer.

The autopsy later revealed that Don had also been subjected to a wash cycle — hot wash, cold rinse. He died long before the spin cycle, which is, I suppose, the only blessing to be had in this entire ugly episode. I am still, to this day, haunted by the mental picture of my grandchild undergoing such brutality. The relentless pounding he received during his forty-five minutes in the dryer is something I would rather not think about. The thought of it visits me like a nightmare! It comes repeatedly to my mind and I put my hands to my head, desperately trying to drive it away. One wishes for an only grandchild to run and play, to graduate from college, to marry and succeed, not to . . . (see, I can't even say it!!!!!!).

The shock and horror that followed Don's death are something I would rather not recount: Calling our children to report the news, watching the baby's body, small as a loaf of bread, as it was zipped into a heavy plastic bag — these images have nothing to do with the merriment of Christmas, and I hope my mention of them will not dampen your spirits at this, the most special and glittering time of the year.

The evening of December sixteenth was a very dark hour for

the Dunbar family. At least with Khe Sahn in police custody we could grieve privately, consoling ourselves with the belief that justice had been carried out.

How foolish we were!!!!!!!!!!!!

The bitter tears were still wet upon our faces when the police returned to Tiffany Circle, where they began their ruthless questioning of Yours Truly!!!!!!!!!!!!! Through the aid of an interpreter, Khe Sahn had spent a sleepless night at police headquarters, constructing a story of unspeakable lies and betrayal! While I am not at liberty to discuss her exact testimony, allow me to voice my disappointment that anyone (let alone the police!) would even *think* of taking Khe Sahn's word over my own. How could I have placed a helpless child in the washing machine? Even if I were cruel enough to do such a thing, when would I have found the time? I was out shopping.

You may have read that our so-called "neighbor" Cherise Clarmont-Shea reported that she witnessed me leaving my home at around one-fifteen on the afternoon of December sixteenth and then, twenty minutes later, allegedly park my car on the far corner of Tiffany and Papageorge and, in her words, "creep" through her backyard and in through my basement door!!!!!! Cherise Clarmont-Shea certainly understands the meaning of the word *creep,* doesn't she? She's been married to one for so long that she has turned into something of a creep herself!! How many times have I opened the door to Cherise, her face swollen and mustard-colored, suffering another of her husband's violent slugfests! She's been smacked in the face so many times she's lucky if she can see anything through those swollen eyes of hers! If the makeup she applies is any indication of her vision, then I believe it is safe to say she can't see two inches in front of her, much less testify to the identity of someone she might think she's seen crossing her yard. She's on pills, everyone knows that. She's desperate for attention and I might pity her under different circumstances. I did not return home early and creep through the Shea's unkept backyard, but even if I had, what possible motive would I have had? Why would I, as certain people have been suggesting, want to murder my own grandchild? This is madness, pure and simple. It reminds me of a recurring nightmare I often have wherein I am desperately trying to defend myself against a heavily armed hand puppet. The grotesque puppet angrily accuses me of spray-painting slogans on his car. I have, of course, done no such thing. "This is insane, preposterous," I think to myself. "This makes no sense," I say, all the while eyeing the loaded weapon in his small hands and praying for this nightmare to end. Cherise Clarmont-Shea has no more sense than a hand puppet. She has three names! And the others who have made statements against me, Chaz Staples and Vivian Taps, they were both at home during a weekday afternoon doing guess what while their spouses were hard at work. What are *they* hiding? I feel it is of utmost importance to consider the source.

These charges are ridiculous, yet I must take them seriously as my very life may be at stake! Listening to a taped translation of Khe Sahn's police statement, the Dunbar family has come to fully understand the meaning of the words "controlling," "vindictive," "manipulative," "greedy," and, in a spiritual sense, "ugly."

Not exactly the words one wishes to toss about during the Christmas season!!!!!!!!!

A hearing has been set for December twenty-seventh and, knowing how disappointed you, our friends, might feel at being left out, I have included the time and address at the bottom of this letter. The hearing is an opportunity during which you might convey your belated Christmas spirit through deed and action. Given the opportunity to defend *your* character I would not hesitate and I know you must feel the exact same way toward me. That heartfelt concern, that desire to stand by your friends and family, is the very foundation upon which we celebrate the Christmas season, isn't it?

While this year's Dunbar Christmas will be seasoned with loss and sadness, we plan to proceed, as best we can, toward that day of days, December twenty-seventh — 1:45 P.M. at The White Paw County Courthouse, room 412.

I will be calling to remind you of that information and look forward to discussing the festive bounty of your holiday season.

Until that time we wish the best to you and yours.

Merry Christmas,

The Dunbars

JAMBOREE

EVER since Dad and Rochelle threw me out I have been staying with my sister and her family. Marty doesn't want me living inside the house proper so I sleep in the garage. He says he wants me back here so I can keep an eye out for the sons of bitches who broke in and sawed the handlebars off his motorcycle.

It's a good thing nobody tried ripping off his shingles — that way he'd have me sleeping on the roof.

Vicki told me I should count my blessings. "There's plenty of people who got it a lot worse than this. People in Europe are living in drainpipes with flies crawling all over their faces. They're eating cardboard and bathing in their own spit. Over in China they have to sleep standing up in muddy ditches. This here," she said, spreading out her arms to indicate majesty, "this here is nothing to look down your nose at. You're living like a king. Look at everything I've done for you."

I looked at the carpet remnants she had laid upon the concrete floor for use as a bed, and at the table she fashioned by placing a board on top of the grill. For decoration she had nailed up a poster picturing a baby orangutan sitting behind a cluttered desk, up to his neck in paperwork. The poster reads "One of these days I've got to get organizized."

I used to think that Vicki had something going for her but now, when I ask myself how I ever got such a notion, I shrug my shoulders and chalk it up to my past ignorance and youth. I was maybe ten years old when Vicki decided, out of nowhere, to join her high school chorus. She auditioned and was accepted, just like that. I can recall listening to her practice all alone in her room, holding a stick of deodorant in place of a microphone. Her voice was nothing special but she never allowed that fact to dampen her spirits. "I'm very much into music. I'm so much into the whole fucking entertainment industry that it practically scares the life out of me. I'm destined for something big, something bigger than the both of us. Something huge." I watched as she stood before the mirror, brushing out her hair and challenging her reflection. "You are a winner, at the top of your game. You call the shots, nobody but you." She would then change her clothes three or four times while discussing her future and all the records she would release. I would observe her, lying on the bed with a stuffed animal and see that as a record cover: *Vicki: The Early Years,* or *Playfully Yours, Vicki!* I had it all worked out.

I figured that, once her career took off, Vicki would go through several managers before turning to me. "Please, Chug. If you want me to beg I will. I need you now because, damn it, you're the only person I can trust." As her manager I would accompany her on all of her concert engagements, where ordinary people would approach her, thrilled and nervous, their faces shiny with admiration. Vicki might sign autographs and pose for snapshots but with the understanding that none of these people could ever be her true friends, only her fans. After a concert we would be led out of the stadium to a waiting tour bus equipped with a refrigerator, bathroom, and comfortable seats that fold into beds when you're ready to call it a night. Vicki would curl up in the seat beside me and whisper, "What do you think of the way I performed 'Love Don't Stand a Chance'? Honestly, Chug, what's your opinion?" Then I would tell her, honestly, taking her fragile personality into consideration. First I would mention that her hair and makeup looked really great. "That satin poncho is a knockout!" I would highlight all the positive aspects, and then, very gently, I might say, "Perhaps at tomorrow night's show it would be a good idea to hold the weeping until the end of the concert."

Vicki would nod her head and remove a small notebook from her tour purse. "Good idea, Chug," she would say. "Excellent suggestion."

The band members would twist in their seats, trying to read what she had written down but Vicki, feeling their watchful eyes, would hold the notebook tight against her chest. They would know damned good and well tomorrow but tonight it's just between Vicki and her brother. And that is what I had always planned to be, her brother. Not in order to grow rich — I never really thought of that. It would be *her* idea to make me her manager — not mine. Of course I would often be surrounded by enthusiastic crowds of people asking, "What's she *really* like?" That would be fun, sure, but only for a little while. I would never have used her as a ploy to get my name in the papers or to put out a record of my own. Far from it. That's something our father would try. He talks like he can smell money from a distance of five miles. He'll see someone wearing a tweed cap and driving a sportscar and say, "Now there's a guy with something in his wallet." That, to me, is like seeing someone on crutches and guessing they have a problem with their leg. Any idiot can do that.

Our father would be the first in line, hoping to cash in on

Vicki's success. He would want his own album or a guest appearance on a television special and Vicki and I would have to spend many long hours explaining that, despite what he may have read in the magazines, it really doesn't work that way. After the way he has treated us it would be both entertaining and embarrassing to hear him say, "But a lot of people just sort of . . . talk through a song. All right, OK, maybe I can't 'sing' but I sure as hell can talk, can't I? C'mon kids, you know I can pull it off. Get me a record, just one. One record for your old dad. I can make it a hit, you know I can. One hit record for Daddy."

Vicki and I would watch him beg. Then we might call in a few record executives and watch him beg some more.

"I could do 'The Man in My Little Girl's Life,' " he would say. "There's all kinds of songs you can do without ever actually having to sing."

"Oh?" the record executive would say. "Name a few others."

Our father would massage his forehead. "Well," he'd say. "There's a lot of them, a whole hell of a lot."

In my mind Vicki and I stand in the doorway watching our father beg for a recording contract. I figure that, to keep from laughing, I will have to bite the inside of my cheeks. Blood will rise up in my throat — that same bitter taste you get after absentmindedly holding a coat hanger in your mouth. Afterwards the record executive will take Vicki and me to lunch at a steak restaurant, where we will recount every moment of our father's pathetic display. "You two are the goddamned salt of the fucking earth," the executive might say, slicing into his twice-baked potato. "But that father of yours, Jesus Christ, what a . . ."

Then Vicki and I would touch hands under the table, hoping that he might come up with the perfect word. I had this all worked out in my mind.

In her second year of high school Vicki dropped out of the chorus because the teacher was an asshole.

"I'm still into music like you wouldn't believe," she said. "But that son of a bitch Yelverton can kiss my rosy red you-know-what if he thinks I'm going to stand in the back row and take part in his bullshit Glen Campbell medley. I don't need that shit and I practically told him that right to his face. I just about said, 'I don't *need* this bullshit.' I was going to say, 'Who the fuck cares about some lonely asshole stringing up telephone lines?' I don't need this kind of bullshit in my life because I've got a career to think about. Hell, Chug, I can write my own goddamned songs and you better believe I will."

She decided to drop out of school altogether because it was too much bullshit and, being a night owl, she hated the hours. She thought she might get herself a job in the music industry. She said it as though there was a thriving music industry in our town. Shortly after dropping out of school Vicki and Dad engaged in a violent argument when one of her boyfriends accidentally set the living room sofa on fire. I sat on the edge of the bed and watched her cram clothing into paper bags. "The day I allow that bald-headed bastard to smack me with a bag full of frozen chicken wings is the day I die," she said, pausing to soothe the bruise on her forehead. "I don't need this kind of bullshit in my life, not anymore. This bird is taking wing. I am out of here, friend." She acted as though there was an airplane in the yard, the pilot tapping his fingers against the face of his watch, waiting. "The next time you hear from me I'll be in California. California or Reno. I'm going to a place where people don't have to live up to their necks in bullshit. This is something I've been thinking about for a long time," she said. "One hell of a long time. Yes, sirree, Vicki has definitely met her quota of bullshit once and for all. It's time to grab the bull by the horns and say, 'Adios, bullshit.' Hand me that clock radio, will you Chug? Your sister is fucking out of here."

It turned out that Vicki did not leave for Reno or California but, instead, for Ginger Treadwell's. Ginger was the boyfriend who had set the sofa on fire, an older red-headed guy who lived three blocks away in a basement apartment he rented from his mother. Every now and then I would go by to visit her but she never came over to the house or phoned as she didn't want to see our father. "Tell him I'm a model and a stewardess and never know where I'll be from one day to the next. And tell him they're making a movie of my life story and they want Boris Fucking Karloff to play his part."

When she broke up with Ginger she moved in with Shane Lambson and then with Drew Hodges, who had a job driving a special bus for crippled people in a hurry. She was living with Drew when she met and fell in love with Marty Manning, a mechanic for the special buses. They dated in secret until she discovered she was pregnant. When he heard the news, Marty lifted his tool box over his head, threw it across the room, and asked for my sister's hand in marriage. Vicki accepted. She said that, with Marty, she felt as though she had woken from a long coma of waste and unhappiness. She wrote a song about it and delivered it at the wedding while Marty accompanied her on drums. He wore a brown tuxedo at the ceremony but removed his jacket for the demanding solo. I couldn't hear a word of Vicki's song. Later on, at the reception, Marty made a speech, telling everyone just how much this new baby meant to him. He knelt down and toasted my sister's stomach, saying, "This lady has given me the greatest gift a man could ever want — a new beginning." He choked up for a moment and then tapped his glass against Vicki's stomach, sloshing punch on her corduroy wedding dress.

It was puzzling that Marty Manning would make such a big production out of this when he already had one New Beginning in his past, a five-year-old daughter he never saw or spoke to. He claims he would love to spend time with Amber but can't because the child's mother is a manipulating ball-buster and a four-star bitch. He said he wanted this baby to be the real thing so he set to work, getting everything ready. He put a bigger sink in the kitchen and made a carseat by sawing the legs off a padded chair. He put locks on a few of the cabinet doors and had Vicki's cat put to sleep. His mother had told him that a cat's instinct is to sneak into the crib and suck the breath out of a newborn baby. It broke my sister's heart but she went along with it. "I have to look toward the future," she said, emptying the litter box for the final time.

I told her she was crazy to let him put her cat to sleep. I said, "Marty sucks, not Sabbath."

Marty was sucking the brains right out of my sister's head. He had her turn the dining room into a nursery. There is a decent-sized spare room down the hall but that is where Marty keeps his drum set and his weights, and he says it is off-limits because it is his domain. He was really banking on a boy but told Vicki to paint the dining room orange just in case. I visited her on that day and wound up painting the room myself while she drank three cans of Tab and asked me questions about Dad, what he was up to with his new girlfriend and how he can stand such a ball-busting four-star bitch. I had just stopped by, curious to see her. I didn't know beforehand that I would be working and I wound up getting a lot of orange paint on my good shoes. Now they are no longer my good shoes, and every time I lace them up I think back on that day when we didn't know anything about the baby waiting to be born. I imagined myself in the future, telling the grown child that I once painted the nursery orange but that it wasn't my idea. I didn't know if the child would be a boy or a girl. Maybe it would like me or maybe not. Maybe I would have gray hair or perhaps I would be bald on top like my father. Who can say what the future holds?

When she was eight months pregnant Vicki lost her job dispatching buses for crippled people because she had to sleep a lot and couldn't make it to work on time. She had someone else punch in for her but they caught on when the buses didn't show up and paralyzed people had to wait in the snow for hours on end. Marty told her not to look for another job until the baby enrolled in the first grade. He had spoken to his mother and said he didn't want anything like those latchkey children. To hear him tell it the Latchkeys were a tough family who lived in his mother's neighborhood and threw rocks at passing cars just for fun. Marty thought he had everything under control.

The baby, a boy named Marty Jr., was born on Thanksgiving Day. Vicki said it was symbolic because Marty Jr., like a pilgrim, was a newcomer to this strange and wonderful country. Also, being a Sagittarian, he would be quick with numbers and get along well with just about everyone but Capricorns, Leos, and Geminis. She tried her best to look on the bright side but still she turned away every time the nurse tried presenting her with the baby, fidgeting in its blanket.

Certain small, ugly creatures are considered adorable and cute. Take, for example, the baby orangutan pictured on the poster that decorates the garage wall. Nothing about this animal is pretty to look at but he doesn't seem to care one way or the other. When an orangutan catches his reflection in a pool of crystal-clear water he doesn't take the time to get depressed about his looks. Instead he just goes about his business, eating leaves and examining the heads of his friends and family, searching for mouthwatering fleas. A creature is cute as long as it has mournful eyes and lives in the woods. An ugly person can't be carefree like the animals. From what I've seen on television, animals will mate without regard to who has a glossier coat or the longest whiskers. I don't get the idea that apes turn down dates. They might talk but I doubt anyone's feelings get hurt in the process. I could be wrong because I am not a scientist. I suppose that some ugly babies can grow up to be OK-looking but I doubt this will be the case with young Marty Jr.

When he was first born my nephew looked like a doll. A doll made of raw hamburger meat. Most babies come that way but it was a lot worse with Marty Jr., who remained raw and blistered after repeated washings. His features continue to look handmade and richly textured. Vicki tried convincing Marty that babies age and grow into their faces. She said his ruddy color meant that he would tan easily later in life.

"He'll be a lady-killer," she said to Marty. "Just like his old man, a four-star lady-killer."

Marty wasn't buying any of it. This child was clearly not

what he had in mind and he regarded it as if it were an oversized turd. His mild curiosity was replaced by disgust and, finally, anger.

"I can tell you're the daddy because he's got your eyes!" a nurse made the mistake of saying to him.

Marty waited until she had taken the baby away before calling the nurse a bitch and repeating "No *I've* got my eyes. *Me* — I have the both of them." He pointed to his face and accidentally stuck his finger into his left eye. When Vicki offered him a Kleenex he brushed her hand away, knocking her water glass to the floor.

"I'm sorry, I'm sorry, I'm sorry." Vicki repeated these words until it was just a noise. Marty turned his back to her until another nurse arrived with her dinner tray. Marty ate everything but the pudding.

When I first laid eyes on Marty Jr. I understood that he would need to develop a winning personality ASAP so, after he was released from the hospital, I quit school in order to help Vicki take care of him. To be honest I probably would have quit anyway so, when Vicki suggested it, I was grateful to have such a formal-sounding excuse. The only person I miss is my English teacher, Mrs. Colgate. She told me to keep in touch and to "read, read, read." I called her once but hung up when she answered the phone crying, "Curtis, listen. For the love of God, Curtis, I can explain everything."

Carrying a baby had worn my sister out. After her week in the hospital she decided that now was the time for Vicki to start thinking about Vicki. This was the time for her to reevaluate and work off the weight she had gained while eating for two. How she worked it off while watching fourteen hours of television a day is anyone's guess — but it worked! I would arrive in the morning and spend my day taking care of the baby: changing and feeding, putting him down for naps, giving him a bath, laundry — I did it all.

"Teach him to cry only during the commercials," Vicki would

shout from the living room whenever he began to fuss. "He needs to spend more time outdoors, that's his problem. Take him to the grocery store and let him look at the meat."

I stayed at the house until the baby was put to bed for the night and then I returned home to my father's place at around nine-thirty in the evening. By this time he understood that Vicki was neither a model nor a stewardess. He wasn't invited to the wedding but didn't seem to mind, saying, "She'll invite me to the next one." He expressed no interest in Marty Jr. "I'm too young to be a grandfather," he said, brushing the sides of his head, the top bald and gleaming.

During Marty Jr.'s nap time I straightened up the house and made a list of the things we needed: clothing, formula, diapers, shampoo — baby things. I carried the list to Vicki, who would keep her eyes fixed on the television and say, every time, "Bring it up with the Bank of America," which meant Marty. And I hated asking him because he always treated it like a loan, implying that I still hadn't paid him back the twenty dollars I hit him up for last week.

This was around the time my father's girlfriend, Rochelle, moved in. Rochelle works as an old waitress and always has money in her purse, a roll of bills the size of a hair curler. When she returns home from work she acts as though she has just walked across the burning desert in her bare feet and has cactus thorns dug deep into her heels. "Now it's my gaddampt time to get waited on," she says, dropping her pocketbook on the kitchen chair and limping off to the living room to put her feet up. She yells at my father, "Change the gaddampt channel and bring me a caffee."

My father yells at me, "Change the goddamned channel and bring Rochelle a coffee."

A remote control would not have solved the problem. Rochelle needed a full-time slave. Every now and then, during one of my trips to the kitchen, fetching her this or that, I would open her purse and take a little something for Marty Jr., just a few dollars here and there for diapers and formula. It was easier than asking Marty and I felt that Rochelle owed me something for my many hours of service.

The baby got by but still there were certain things that cost more than the few dollars a day I was able to provide. Special things, such as a rabbit-fur jacket that caught his eye one afternoon in a shop window. I wrote these things down as they came to me and posted the list on the refrigerator, where Marty would be forced to notice it. A few days before the baby's first birthday I was in the dining room when I heard the sound of paper being crumpled. Then I heard Marty call out, "What was that shit on the refrigerator?"

Vicki was on the living room sofa and answered him saying, "What shit?"

Marty said, "You know what shit I'm talking about."

Vicki didn't say anything.

"You know I can't stand to have shit taped to my refrigerator."

Vicki said, "No, sir, I didn't know that."

"Well, you know it now, don't you?"

Vicki said, "I guess I do."

For his birthday I decorated with balloons and bought Marty Jr. a store-bought cake and a stuffed E.T. with some of Rochelle's stolen money. The cake he threw up. The E.T. scared him until I blacked out its keen eyes with a Magic Marker. We celebrated by ourselves as Vicki and Marty chose to spend their Thanksgiving with someone named Cuff Daniels, a guy Marty used to jam with. For his birthday they gave their son a wishbone from the turkey they had eaten. Vicki carried it home in her purse and it was covered in lint.

As Christmas neared I made another list and worked up the nerve to approach Marty man-to-man about the gifts his son deserved. Marty regarded the list for a moment before folding it in half. He told me that Christmas is just another day as far as a baby is concerned. He folded the list again, explaining that, as far as he was concerned, Christmas had nothing to do with spending all your hard-earned money on bullshit gifts.

"Christmas is in here," he said, pointing to the spot where he thought his heart might be. "It's on the inside, where it counts." He folded the paper again and again until it was the size of a matchbook, all the while telling me some story about the time someone's Christmas tree caught their house on fire and he found a roll of quarters in the ashes. The money had melted into a lump and he used it as a paperweight until some asshole stole it off his worktable.

For Christmas Marty bought himself a motorcycle, brand-new. He gave Vicki a helmet, unwrapped. He just handed it to her. The two of them rode off to Cuff Daniels's house and brought the baby another wishbone. This one still had meat on it and was ice-cold from riding in Vicki's pocket.

For the first few months Marty parked his motorcycle in the dining room nursery. He would take it out for joyrides and guide it back into the house, where he would lay newspapers on the floor and tinker with it. Marty understood that enclosed exhaust fumes can be fatal so he was always careful to raise all the windows while the engine was running. It was a nuisance as I would turn my back for a moment and discover the baby sitting on the greasy newspaper with a wrench in his mouth, the cold air steaming from his nose.

I bided my time, waiting for the day Marty would park the motorcycle in the garage rather than forcing it up the front steps of the house. I knew the day would come and when it finally arrived, a Thursday evening in early February, I sneaked into the garage with a hacksaw. It took me four hours in the dark but I did it: I sawed off both the handlebars. I also filled the gas tank with Dr. Pepper, but Marty is so caught up in the handlebars he still hasn't noticed it. The next morning, when Vicki told me what had happened, I acted shocked. She led me to the garage, where she pointed to a scattering of metal flakes on the concrete floor.

"There," she said, aiming with her cigarette. "Those are the shavings."

When Marty came home from work he did the same thing, led me to the garage and pointed out the shavings. He told me there was no use in calling the police seeing as they've had it in for him since day one. Marty said he would solve this crime himself, one man, on his own. He said he couldn't say for sure but he was practically certain that Cuff Daniels had something to do with it. "Good old Cuff," he said. Then he spit on the concrete floor.

Things went along like always until the next week, when Rochelle caught me taking money from her purse. Normally I could always tell where she was as I could hear her moaning, sometimes actual words and other times just sounds, like a weary motor. She must have held her breath this time. Maybe she suspected something was up. I turned around and there she was.

"I wasn't taking your money," I said, rolling up the bills and replacing the rubber band that held them. "I wasn't taking it, I was just . . . counting it. You've got thirty-seven dollars here. Boy, that's a lot of tips, thirty-seven dollars."

Rochelle stood in the doorway with her fists in the air. "Not but twenty minutes ago I had forty-one dollars," she said, hobbling closer toward me. "Do you expect me to believe that the rest of my money got tired of being cooped up in that packetbook and decided to walk off on its own and explore the world? Is that what you expect me to believe? Is it? Because, let me tell you something, Mister, I can't stand a thief."

She brought her fist up against the side of my face. "Somebody needs to box your ears, Mister, and it might as well be me because if there's one thing I can't stand it's a thief, a lazy, sneaking thief."

She kept hitting me, her voice rising until my father came from the bathroom and pulled her off of me. After listening to her side of the story he calmly placed his left hand on my shoulder and, with his right, punched me very hard in the stomach.

"That's what he needs," Rochelle said, "someone to box his ears. Thief! Liar."

Just like Vicki before me, I packed my belongings into paper bags. At the time all I felt was shame and regret — not for taking the money, but for my pitiful lie that I was just counting it. I know how I must have looked at that moment, washed out and sneaky and stupid. I should have said I was collecting for services rendered and stood my ground. I should have predicted my father's punch. Should have, should have. I spent the night in the woods behind my father's house thinking of all the should haves. That night I should have packed a sleeping bag.

The following morning I presented my case to Vicki, who said she'd bring it up with Marty when the time was right. I spent the next two nights in their backyard before he decided I could stay in the garage. It doesn't have any heat but at least it's dry. I ran an extension cord in from the house so now I can choose between having a lamp or the broken TV, which has sound but no picture, just a snowy gray screen that I find I can't take my eyes off.

Marty Jr. can walk now. He can even think. If you point and say, "Bring me the book, Baby, bring me the book," he will do it. When you ask, "Where's Big Bird?" Marty Jr. will toddle over and pound on the TV set, hoping to drive him out. He's not stupid — far from it. Soon he will speak and I have been working to coach him. Everything I touch I hold up and name in an instructive tone of voice. "Cushion," I'll say. "Ashtray." "Can opener." I do this only in the daytime, when Marty's not around. Last Sunday, at dinner, he started making fun of me. He picked up his fork and turned to the baby saying, "Douche Bag." Then he pointed at me and said, "Dip Shit. Dip Shit."

Marty Jr. clapped his hands together and said, "Dishyt, Dishyt."

I thought Vicki and Marty would never stop laughing. They patted Marty Jr. on the head, and he said it again: "Dishyt." It burned me up that he might turn on me like that. He said it once more while I was putting him to bed and I took the meat of his thigh and twisted it between my fingers.

A few weeks after I moved in, Marty caught the baby making a long-distance call. It was just dumb luck — he punched in some numbers and made a connection. When Marty took the phone out of the baby's hand, he found himself speaking to a woman who kept saying, *"C'est toi, Julien? . . . C'est toi?"*

Marty thought the baby had dialed China. Vicki said it sounded like Hawaii to her.

Marty said, "Hawaii, China, or Puerto Rico, what the hell difference does it make? I'm the one who's stuck paying for it and, in case you haven't noticed, I am not made of money. Is that what you thought, that I'm made of money?"

Vicki said, "No, sir, I do not."

Marty Jr., on a roll, gurgled and dialed 911.

The next day Marty placed all the telephones in high places, where the baby couldn't reach them. Then he went out and got himself a dog. A puppy might have been nice for the baby but Marty brought home a full-grown Doberman, a used dog given to him by a guy he works with. Jamboree has a bullet head and a stumpy tail, like a big black thumb smeared with shit. I think perhaps the previous owner trained him to be unpleasant. I've seen that in a magazine before, men with thick pads around their arms, provoking dogs to attack so they can qualify for high-paying jobs patrolling department stores and car lots. Jamboree was here only two days before he took down Playboy, the neighbor's old basset hound. Poor Playboy didn't know what hit him. Marty took the body and set it in the street, hoping his owners would believe Playboy had been hit by a car.

Right, Marty, a car with teeth.

Jamboree shouldn't be allowed on the street, even on a leash. Everyone but Marty is afraid of this dog. Even cars speed up when they see him on the sidewalk. During the night Jamboree sleeps on a pad beside his master's bed. Vicki told me that she no longer drinks fluids after 9:00 P.M. as she is afraid to leave the bed and risk going to the bathroom. Jamboree has already bitten her once, nipped her when she tried to remove an ashtray from the mattress. Marty tells her that Jamboree can smell her fear and that she has no one but herself to blame for being a coward. Vicki asked him what her fear smells like and he said it stinks like a carton of milk left out in the sun for five days to a week.

"Where's my champ? Where is he? Where's my boy?" Marty will ask, and Jamboree will come kneeling before him, the stump of a tail moving back and forth, hitching for a ride.

After he leaves for work in the morning, Vicki and I coax the dog into the spare room and shut the door. Then I take the baby out of his crib and carry on about my business. We can all hear Jamboree passing time in the spare room, whining and scratching at the door. At first I was afraid Marty Jr., curious, would open the door but he's smart; he knows what's in there.

My fear smells like damp wood, so I built Marty Jr. a playpen. I made it myself with my own two hands. When Marty returns from work he lets the dog loose and I set Marty Jr. in his pen, where I hope he might be safe. Jamboree circles around, trying to get at him but Marty Jr. is smart and knows to keep back from the bars. He stands in the center of his pen, watching. Once in a while he'll throw something over the top. Last night Jamboree ate E.T. The dining room floor was littered with tufts of plush fur and Styrofoam BBs.

This morning I set Marty Jr.'s crib atop a platform — a dining room table I found in the neighbor's trash pile. I stood on a chair and settled him in, thinking he might marvel at this new perspective. "Look at you," I said. "On top of the world." He cried then and when I went to comfort him he grabbed my hair and didn't let go until I popped him across the face. I tell myself that it's not his fault, that things will be different when it's just the two of us on our own. And it will be different. I found the place where Marty hides his money. There's close to three hundred dollars here, enough to take the baby and me to Florida, where it's warm. We can camp out there, live in the woods until I get a job. Marty would have the national guard on my ass if I were to poison his dog, but I don't think he'll care one way or another if I take off with his son. And Vicki — she might think about it for a week or so, and then she'd let it go, saving it up for a year or two down the road, when she'll turn to the person sitting beside her at the tavern and say, "Did I ever tell you about the time my very own brother ran off with my fucking baby? Did I?"

7

:45. I ARRIVE at Malison's hotel an hour and fifteen minutes before his lecture is due to begin at the Pavilion of Thought. The desk clerk shoots me a look that suggests he might be interested in throwing his weight around. Rather than pass him, I take a seat in the lobby, pull out my journal, and light a cigarette. He gives me another look.

"My husband hates for me to smoke in the room," I say.

He says, "What?"

I say, "My husband, he hates the smoke, so I'm just going to sit here for a moment before going up to our room."

The clerk says, "Fine, whatever," and turns his attention back to a little TV set, one of those Watchmans.

I can't believe that Malison is staying here at The Chesterton. It's so ironic, so unlike Malison. It's perfect. I'd called every hotel in town asking if they had a Malison registered, but of course they didn't. We're not talking about Mr. Small Press Nobody here. Malison is MALISON, and he's got to protect his privacy. I can understand that. I can respect that. I called around again asking if anyone had a guest by the name of Smithy Smithy, the name of all the characters in Malison's second novel. All the hotel clerks said no. They said, "What the hell kind of name is that?" Really, I think Smithy Smithy would have been too obvious, so I tried again and again, thinking he might have registered under the name of one of the minor characters in *Rotunda Surf*. I finally found him here at The Chesterton registered under the name A. Davenport, the character who undergoes a needless colostomy in *Magnetic Plugs*. Malison is here in room 822.

How like Malison to use an assumed name, and especially here at The Chesterton, where he'll be rubbing elbows with every shallow middle-class cliché you'd never want to meet, the exact type of people he exposes in his novels. How like Malison, how perfectly ironic.

8:04. I had really hoped to catch Malison before he left for the reading, but since nobody answers his door I can only assume that the department heads have him hog-tied at The Crow's Nest or Andrea's Butcher Block, one of the upscale slaughterhouses this town calls a restaurant. I can see it now: the dean and his spaniels are shoveling forkfuls of red meat while poor Malison just sits there, tuning out their petty conversation and gagging at the sight of the carnage on his plate. Even the vegetables in this town are cooked in blood. I think it's pretty obvious that the English Department knows nothing about Malison. They just see him as another feather in their cap, a name they can use to attract new students. It makes me sick. They fly him in for a few days, race him around campus like a greyhound, and then bore him to death with their talk of funding cutbacks and

Who's Who on campus. I've been standing outside this door for the last twenty minutes, so I think it's also very obvious that they're herding Malison straight from the restaurant to the Pavilion of Thought.

At first I was excited about tonight's reading, but now I say forget it — if Malison has been rushed around by these university types all day, then I know he'll be too exhausted to express himself. I had a feeling this might happen, so I arranged for a few people to tape tonight's reading at the Pavilion. Bethany, if left to her own devices, can tend to get a little too artsy for her own good, so I got Daryll as a backup. Deep down in his middle-class heart Daryll would just love to be a cameraman for some big TV studio. He'd love to wear a jumpsuit and boss people around. While I really hate his politics, I trust his overall skill much more than I trust Bethany's. She taped last month's John Cage lecture and kept the camera aimed at his feet the entire time, and he wasn't dancing or anything!

Another reason for boycotting tonight's lecture is that I don't think I can sit back and watch while Malison wastes his time reading to an audience of a thousand kids who can't even begin to understand his work. The students began lining up outside the Pavilion hours ago. They're holding Malison's book in one hand and some bullshit economics text in the other, economics or political science or whatever it is they're *really* interested in. Most of them had never even heard of Malison before *Rotunda Surf,* but they act as though they've been reading Malison forever. I want to confront them. I want to ask them where they were when Malison was physically attacked after the release of *Magnetic Plugs.* Where were *they* when Malison needed support after the media trashed *Smithy Smithy?* These kids all act like they understand Malison and it makes me sick to hear their lame opinions on his work. This afternoon I overheard a girl telling her boyfriend that Malison's work mirrored the oppression inherent in Western capitalist society. She read that off the dust jacket. She doesn't know shit about Malison. She was wearing clothes that Malison would really hate. Here at the university I am surrounded by jokes like her.

My head is still spinning from the reading Malison gave in my master's writing seminar this afternoon. I'd looked forward to some one-on-one contact, but the room was packed with people who aren't even enrolled in the seminar. These kids weren't writers, they were fakes. But did the teacher ask them to leave? Did Professor Nobody tell them that this was a class for serious writers? Of course not. He masks his cowardice with this "we're all here to learn" cheeriness that really makes me sick. It was perfect then when Malison walked into the classroom. He saw all the copies of O'Flannery on our desks and he picked up *my* copy and said, "Who's making you read this shit?" It was so perfect. Professor Nobody just stood there pretending he hadn't heard Malison's remark. He just stood there and tucked in his shirt. He couldn't even own up to it! I think Malison hates O'Flannery for the same reasons I do, because she's a fascist, a typical bourgeois racist, a judgmental Christian right-wing parrot, and a timid writer who relies on grammar to carry her through the page. I hate O'Flannery, I really do.

Malison's reading was wonderfully assertive. He read a few sections from *Rotunda Surf,* parts that I had practically memorized even though the book only came out last month. He never numbers his pages, but I was with him for a good quarter-inch at the beginning of the second part. I just mouthed the words while he read. I wasn't doing it for attention; it's just a reflex action because I know his work, all of it, so well. After the reading, Professor Nobody opened the floor for questions, which was a mistake because it's always the stupidest people who ask the most questions. For example, one guy who's not even *in* the writing seminar raised his hand and said, "I tried reading your third novel but gave up when I realized that all of the characters were going by the name Smithy Smithy. I found it confusing; I had a real problem with it."

Oh right, *he* had a problem with it.

Malison was great. He just looked at this guy and said, "Well, if it's giving *you* trouble, then I guess I'll just have to rewrite it in simpler terms. I thought I might continue work on my new project, but if *Smithy Smithy* confuses you, then I guess it's back to the drawing board." Everyone laughed but you could tell that they had problems with *Smithy Smithy* too. I didn't laugh because I don't have any problems with it. I have no problems with Malison. Bethany raised her hand and asked Malison if he had grown up in New York City, which of course he had. It's right there in his writing, and besides, it says so on the back of all his books. Malison answered her; he just said yes, but in a bored way that acknowledged the dumbness of the question. It really was a stupid question and I laughed when she asked it. I was the only one laughing, which simply proves how well I know Malison's life. He gave me a little glance, a little smile, when I laughed. I've spent a lot of time in New York City, and I'm often asked that same question myself. I wasn't raised there, but I could have been. I'm incredibly street-smart.

The questions continued and were all incredibly stupid until I asked Malison if the tall blond character in *Rotunda Surf* was based on his former girlfriend Cassandra Lane, the fashion model. I just wanted Malison to realize that there are some of us who understand his life and work. My New York friend Russell Marks had gone to the Foxmore Academy with Cassandra Lane, and he used to fill me in on a lot of details, like what a bitch she really is and how she uses people. Cassandra Lane really put Malison through the wringer over that phony abuse scandal. She'll do anything for media attention. She's not even that pretty.

I asked the question, and Malison looked at me with a lot of pain, a great deal of pain and anguish in his eyes, and said that *Rotunda Surf* was a work of fiction and that his inspirations were none of anyone's business. A group of people laughed when he said that. I laughed too because I know that, on the surface, my question sounded nosy, but I didn't mean it that way. I realize it would have been impossible for him to open up and really talk about his work in that atmosphere, surrounded by so

many people who don't know him the way I do. I can understand Malison's creative process and his life, and that's why I really need to sit down and talk with him. I saw that pain in his
eyes. I need to sit him down and let him know that I'm behind
him one hundred percent.

After a few more questions, Professor Nobody asked Malison
where he saw this postmodern metafictional movement headed,
and Malison just picked up his books and papers and said,
"Anywhere but here," and walked out of the room. He meant
anywhere but the small world of academia, but it went right
over everyone's head. After he walked out, I picked up my shit
and walked out too, but Malison had already left the building. I
haven't been able to find him anywhere.

9:19. I'm sitting in the cocktail lounge of The Chesterton, a
grotesque, brassy place ironically named Reflections, which erro-
neously suggests that I will see myself mirrored in this bar or any
of its customers. I sit at a table, pull out my journal, and, when
the waitress arrives, I order a boilermaker. The waitress acts
shocked that a woman might order a beer and a shot rather than
some frozen daiquiri product, and I shoot her a look that sends
her off toward a group of people she thinks might find her cute.

Malison's reading is starting right at this moment, I can sense
it. I think it's very appropriate, very revealing that right now he
is standing before an audience of people who don't understand
him, and at the same time I'm sitting in this bar full of people
who, I am certain, have no hope of ever knowing or understanding me. It's a lonely feeling, but I'd rather be alone than stoop to
a lower level of understanding. The waitress brings me my shot
and my beer and gives me a look while I empty the shot glass
into the beer. She acts as though I'm spoiling all her fun.
Whatever fun she might have working in a place like this, leading her dull, unexamined life, she is more than welcome to.
She can have it. The customers are all looking at me the same
way. They can't deal with anyone who isn't into their Mr. and
Mrs. Jovial scene, with someone who takes a hard look at the

crumbling building blocks that are the foundation for their wasted suburban lives. With someone like me.

This place reminds me of the bar that Malison depicted in *Magnetic Plugs*, except the people are fully dressed and they're not drinking out of gas cans. The waitress returns and I order another boilermaker.

10:20. I'm sitting in the fancy lounge area of the women's rest room here at The Chesterton. I shouldn't have had that champagne on top of those boilermakers, but if I sit very quietly I'm sure I can pull myself together. Actually, I'm not even embarrassed about throwing up in the bar. I was having problems putting my feelings into words, so vomiting was actually a very ironic, very appropriate gesture. I'm not going to let it get me down, but still I curse that crippled man for distracting me the way he did. Malison's lecture is probably over by now, and he'll be heading back to his room. Thank God I brought that change of clothes. It's not my favorite outfit but, seeing as my first choice is spattered with vomit, I guess I'll have to go with the second choice.

That old guy is probably still sitting in the bar, using his napkin to mop up the vomit and trying to convince the waitress that the world is good at heart. He'd come over to my table and asked to join me, and I looked up from my writing and said, "Go ahead, sit down," not because I wanted company, but because he obviously needed to sit someplace and all the other chairs were taken. This man walked with two canes and his legs were twisted. Each foot pointed off in a different direction as though they had been attached sideways. He sat down and asked the waitress to bring us her finest bottle of champagne. The waitress asked, "What are you celebrating?" and the man just spread out his arms and looked back and forth across the room. I said, "You're celebrating this bar?" and he said, "No, I'm celebrating life!" I should have gotten up and left; but instead I saw this man as someone I can use for a piece I'm working on. He's someone whom Malison would describe as a self-hypnotic, one of those people who convinces himself that his life is meaningful only because the truth would destroy him. It's as if someone has hypnotized him by waving a turd back and forth in front of his face and saying, "You're getting sleepy . . . sleepy."

When the champagne arrived at the table, the crippled man grinned from ear to ear. And I mean that literally. He had the widest mouth I have ever seen on a human. I think he could have fit a saucer in there with no problem. He had this wide mouth and sandy blond hair growing in tufts along the sides of his head. The top of his head was bald and covered with spots and freckles. He made a big production of popping the cork off the champagne bottle, and the people at the other tables all looked our way and cheered him on. Everyone acted as if this were important and memorable. The man poured two glasses and then noticed my journal and said, "So, I see you're a writer." This would be like me noticing his two canes leaning against the table and saying, "So, I see you're a cripple," but I bit my tongue and just said, "Yes, I'm a writer." The man said he'd never written much besides letters but that reading was his greatest pleasure. Then he rattled off a list of the writers he admired — fussy, middle-of-the-road contemporaries — and I said, "Aren't all those people dead?" and he grabbed at his heart and said, "I hope not!" It went right over his head. He asked who I like reading, and when I answered, "Malison," he winced. You'd think I'd spat in his drink. It pissed me off. I don't need this man's approval to read *anything.* I'm not here to live up to his expectations. I'd rather die than live up to his expectations. His attitude was getting on my nerves, and I should have just packed up my shit and left. I asked if he'd actually read any of Malison's work, and he said as a matter of fact, yes, he had. He said he'd recently found himself on a Greyhound bus to St. Louis and had discovered too late that the attaché case containing all his books had been stored below along with his luggage. He said he'd spent eight hours reading a copy of *Rotunda Surf* he'd found abandoned on the seat beside him. He used that word, *abandoned,* to suggest that someone had deliberately walked away from a hardcover Malison.

This man proceeded to question what he called Malison's "defensiveness" and said he doubted the wisdom of *Rotunda Surf's* prologue. It is supremely ironic that this man, this joker with the canes and the wide mouth, would question Malison. Who does he think he is? That prologue is one of my favorite parts of the whole book. In it Malison writes: "If you, reader, can yank your head out of your own asshole long enough to finish the first chapter, don't make the mistake of congratulating yourself. You possess nothing but fleeting, momentary courage. The shit on your face is still wet. It is your mask." It is so true, but I could see that this crippled guy couldn't digest it at all because Malison was directing the prologue at people just like him — people who wear masks. While I respected this wide-mouthed man for taking the chance to break out of his mindless existence, I could see that he hadn't taken a hard enough look at Malison's world. He poured us some more champagne, and I said that I didn't think it was Malison's job to create a comfortable world for escapists, some flowery paradise where Mr. and Mrs. America could walk hand-in-hand and think of themselves as wonderful people. Malison's whole point is that hardly anyone is a wonderful person. There was a reason all the characters in *Rotunda Surf* had transparent bodies: most people *are* transparent. Malison can see right through middle-class people, and so can I. Some of us just have that ability. Malison and I are the type of writers who will always be on the outside looking in. Looking in but not banging to be let in. We don't want in if it means we'll have to pay the price by becoming as shallow and transparent as everyone else.

The crippled man couldn't handle this at all. He said, "No one on this earth is transparent. Not even us." I thought he was talking about himself and the other people in the bar, and I felt sorry for him. Then it hit me he was referring to himself and me. He put us in the same boat when we're not even in the same fucking ocean. He said that we're lucky to live in a world populated with unique, complex people. That was when I lost it and threw up on the table. It was perfect timing. All those people who had watched him pop the cork looked our way again but with a different sort of expression on their faces. I just grabbed my shit and ran out, ran into the rest room in the lobby.

Luckily I've brought a change of clothes. The fresh outfit was in my duffel bag along with a hairbrush, flat shoes, my tooth-brush, all of Malison's books, a Walkman, tapes of several of Malison's readings, the last three term papers I wrote on his last three novels (scarred with the ludicrous comments of my teach-ers), copies of all the supportive letters I've written Malison over the years, some dope, two Valiums, my diaphragm, all the short stories I've written since I was fifteen, my novel in progress (which I really need his opinion on), some Scotch tape, and the solution for my contact lenses. I'm not taking any chances tonight!

11:22. I've been standing in the hallway outside Malison's hotel room for the last half-hour rereading my favorite passages of *Magnetic Plugs* and *Smithy Smithy*. His lecture must have ended by now, and I fear they are holding him hostage with another mindless question-and-answer session. My God, how much do they expect him to take?!

He'd looked so tired when I saw him this afternoon before my master's class. I'd left my desk and was on my way to the bathroom when I passed him in the hall. It was incredible. The air was charged. Malison was wearing a pair of camouflage fa-tigues and a sports coat made of something rough, something like burlap. I thought he had silver hair, but up close I could see it was kind of a flat gray color, a color I like a lot more than sil-ver. His eyelids were dark and puffy because the department heads had tired him out, but the eyes themselves were a rare in-tense shade of brown, like two clean pennies shining. Malison was walking toward the classroom with Brouner, the depart-ment head, who was running off at the mouth about his favorite subject — himself. Brouner was saying, "You might have heard of me. I had an essay on art and analysis in last month's *Forefront*," and Malison said, "If you've been published in *Forefront*, then no, I haven't heard of you." Malison is so blunt, so matter-of-fact, so uninterested in playing games. He wouldn't be caught dead reading *Forefront*.

I tried to catch his eye in the hallway. I wanted to let him know that everyone knows what an asshole Brouner is, but then Professor Nobody came up and started yapping at me about my overdue essay, and Malison was herded into an office. I can't imagine what's keeping him now. If I know Malison, he's fed up with the English Department; he's not going to jump through any more of their hoops. Where could he be? I'll wait here for a few more minutes, and if he doesn't show, then I'll head over to the Pavilion of Thought. The suspense is killing me.

12:09. I'm standing in a sheltered bus stop on west campus waiting for this fucking rain to let up so I can return to the hotel. The Pavilion of Thought was empty when I arrived. The show was over. I was on my way back to the hotel when I ran into Bethany in front of the Rathskeller, where she was taking potshots at people with her video camera (as if that hasn't been done thousands of times before). Bethany started in about the Malison reading. She said, "Where were you? My God, you missed it. I don't believe you." Sometimes Bethany takes a very cocky, very inside attitude that infuriates me. She lies a lot, too. Sometimes I don't even think she realizes she's lying. She took this superior attitude and told me that just before tonight's reading Malison approached her, bummed a cigarette, and passed some time with her.

Right, Bethany.

She said that Malison said he'd remembered her from the master's class and that he'd like to read her work someday.

Right, Bethany.

Then she told me that he read a chapterlike passage from a new work in progress, and I covered my ears because whatever it is, I don't want to hear it from Bethany. She is an abysmal storyteller and I don't want Malison's work chewed by her translation. She said she had the lecture on videotape but that no tape could capture the intensity of the reading. She said I can watch the tape but I probably won't be able to understand it, not having been there in person.

This attitude of hers really makes me sick. *I* might not be able to understand Malison? *Me?* This is very ironic, especially coming from Bethany, who had never even heard of Malison before I loaned her my copy of *Smithy Smithy* last semester. *I* might not be able to understand it?

So I said, "Bethany, Malison is *my* writer, and I think I could understand him if he were speaking Egyptian." And she said, "I didn't realize you owned any writers, Anastasia. Are there any others in your stable?" *Stable* is a familiar word to Bethany. Before I turned her on to Malison, she was wearing fucking jodhpurs to class, arranging her hair into a French braid, and drawing horse profiles in the margins of her notebook. Before I turned her on to Malison, Bethany's writing consisted of florid little sentences beginning with "'Tis" and "Oftimes," as if she'd been writing with a fucking quill that she dipped into an inkwell while sitting on an embroidered chair bathed in soft candlelight. Then, overnight she started writing like Malison and going out of her way to mention his name in class. Then in critique she trashed my story, saying that my writing is obviously based on Malison. I was writing like Malison before I even knew who Malison was. I've always written like Malison, so I said, "Maybe Malison is writing like me," and she said (in front of the whole class), she said, "And *where* exactly would Malison have read any of *your* work?" She's so full of herself since she had that story published in *Post-Plane*. Who reads *Post-Plane*?

Bethany is so transparent. I'm sure if Malison did talk to her he only did it in order to get a feel for the stupidity of his audience. She told me she'd invited him out for a postlecture drink, but he'd said he needed to get right back to New York because his wife was expecting a baby. This was just an excuse to get rid of Bethany. Malison was lying, giving her the shake. I know, because Russell Marks told me that he saw Malison's wife, Teresa Compton, at a restaurant in New York City two months ago, and Mark told me that it looked like Teresa Compton had lost weight. Lost weight! How pregnant can she be? Mark also told me that Malison and Teresa are filing for a divorce and living in separate apartments, so I highly doubt she's pregnant. Malison was just throwing up a smoke screen to protect himself from Bethany. I know this for a fact because directly after talking to Bethany I called The Chesterton and asked them if A. Davenport had checked out. I had them connect me to Room 822. When Malison answered, I hung up. I didn't want to introduce myself over the phone, so I politely hung up, and if this rain doesn't stop within the next sixty seconds I'm going to say to hell with it and run back to that hotel, rain or no rain.

12:54. I'm back at The Chesterton, in the lounge area of the women's rest room, waiting for my hose to dry. I've got them stuffed into the chute of the hot-air hand dryer, and it's very annoying because women keep coming in here and giving me a hard time about it. Let them dry their hands on their skirts, it won't kill them. Who are they? My second outfit is soaking wet, so I'm back in my original choice. I rinsed most of it out earlier in the evening, and you can hardly notice any vomit except on my blouse. If I thought that one of these women had an ounce of compassion I would ask to borrow a shot of perfume that would solve the lingering odor problem, but understanding seems to be in short supply here at The Chesterton. I've redone my makeup and used the hot-air hand dryer on my hair before putting the hose in. It's hard to style your hair when you're leaning over like that. It came out looking very '70s, a sort of Jerry Hall over-the-shoulder thing, but I guess I'll have to live with it.

Later. I knock on Malison's door, room 822. I can hear the television very ironically tuned to The Hour of Prayer, so I know he's in there. I knock a little harder and am embarrassed when, after my fifth round — and I'm really pounding away — I hear the toilet flush. I hate it when that happens, I really do. I take a step back and compose myself and look down at the carpet, and someone answers the door but it's not Malison. It's that man from the bar, the man with the two canes, and he's relying on them and grinning like a carved pumpkin. And the worst part, the most revolting part of it all, is that he doesn't seem the least bit surprised to see me.

BARREL FEVER

SHORTLY after my mother died, my sisters and I found ourselves rummaging through a cabinet of papers marked "POISON," and it was there, tucked between the pages of a well-worn copy of *Mein Kampf,* that I discovered fifteen years' worth of her annual New Year's resolutions. She took up the practice the winter after my father died, the same year she found a job and bought her first rifle. Every Christmas afternoon, after placing the artificial tree back into its box, she would grow reflective. "Do you think I overuse the word 'nigger'?" she would ask. "Was it wrong of me to spit on that Jehovah's Witness girl? Tell me the truth here. I need a second opinion."

On New Year's Eve she would sit

with her notes and a coffee cup of champagne, glancing at her watch and tapping a pencil against the legs of her chair. She would write something on an index card and, moments later, shake her head and erase it. The process was repeated until she wore a hole through the card and was forced to start fresh on another.

The next morning I would ask, "So, what was on your list, Mom?"

"Smother those homely teenagers who call themselves my children is at the top. Why do you ask?"

"No reason."

I always got a great kick out of my mother, but my sisters, for one reason or another, failed to get the joke. They have grown to be humorless and clinically sensitive: the sorts of people who overuse the words "rage" and "empowerment" and constantly ask, "What do you *really* mean by that?" While I would often call and visit our mother, they kept their distance, limiting their postal or telephone contact to the holidays.

"Did I tell you what your sister Hope sent me for my birthday?" my mother asked during one of our late-night phone calls. "A poncho. Who does she think I am that I might want a poncho? I've written her back saying I'm sure it will come in very handy the next time I mount my burro for the three-day journey over the mountains to the neighboring village. Poncho, indeed. I've thrown it into the garage-sale box along with the pepper grinder Joy sent me. The thing is two feet long, black and shiny — what do I need with a thing like that? It doesn't take a psychiatrist to recognize that pepper grinder for what it truly is. I bet she spent weeks knocking that one around with her therapist. And, oh, it arrived in a fancy box wrapped in tissue paper. You can bet she paid out the ass for it but that's Joy for you, thinking she can impress people with the money she makes 'consulting.' That's what she calls herself now, a consultant, as if that means anything. Anyone who answers questions can call themselves a consultant, am I wrong? A telephone operator is a consultant, a palm reader: they're all consultants. I thought I'd seen it all but then Faith sent me a subscription to that trade paper she's working for. She calls it a magazine. Have you seen it? Why would anyone subscribe to a magazine devoted to adobe? Is this a big trend? Is there something I've missed? I've got a house made of bricks but who wants to read about it every month? Adobe? She circled her name on the first page where she's listed as 'Features Editor.' When people ask what she's up to I always tell them she's a secretary — it sounds better. So then, a week after my birthday I got a call from your sister Charity . . ."

Faith, Hope, Joy, Charity, and me, Adolph.

See, she just couldn't help herself.

While my mother might threaten a yard sale she was not the type of person to invite people onto her property or make change. Following her death my sisters were horrified to discover, sealed in boxes, every gift they had given her.

"How could she *not* want a first edition by M. Scott Peck?"

"I made these wind chimes with my own two hands. Didn't that count for anything?"

"What did she have against pepper grinders?"

Aside from a few stiff wallets fashioned in summer camp, there was nothing of mine in those boxes as, at an early age, I discovered that postage stamps, cartons of cigarettes, light bulbs, and mail-order steaks are the gifts that keep giving.

"How could she possibly be so cruel?" my sisters asked, coming upon the unmailed notes and letters stored in the "POISON" file. "I am not the 'missing link,' I am not, I am *not*," Joy chanted, holding a draft of her graduation card. "I am *not* 'God's gift to fraternity beer baths,' I am not, I am not, I am not." Charity and Faith gathered round and the three of them embraced in a circle of healing. There were letters to me, comparing me unfavorably to both Richard Speck and the late Stepin Fetchit, but in all honesty it really didn't bother me too much. We all entertain hateful thoughts every now and then, and afterwards they either grow stronger or fade away. From one day to the next, in tiny ways, our opinions change or, rather, *my* opinions change. Some of them anyway. That's what makes me either weak or open-minded, depending on what it was I promised the last time we talked. I'm sure that Richard Speck had his share of good qualities and Stepin Fetchit was a terrific dancer, so I try not to take it too hard. My mother hadn't mailed those letters; she simply left them to be discovered after her death. Hey, at least she was thinking about us.

I have posted some of my mother's notes on my refrigerator alongside a Chinese take-out menu and a hideously scripted sympathy card sent by my former friend, Gill Pullen. Sympathy and calligraphy are two things I can definitely live without. Gill Pullen I cannot live without or, rather, I am having to learn to live without. At the risk of appearing maudlin or sentimental it was mutually understood that, having enjoyed each other's company for seven years, we were close. Seeing as he was my only friend, I suppose I could go so far as to call him my best friend. We had our little fights, sure we did. We'd get on each other's nerves and then lay low for a couple of days until something really good came on television, prompting one of us to call the other and say, "Quick — outstanding IV on channel seven." IV stands for innocent victim, usually found shivering on the sidewalk near the scene of the tragedy. The impact of the IV is greater when coupled with the Wind-Blown Reporter, a staple of every news team. Prizewinning IVs have no notion of vanity or guile. Their presence is pathetic in itself but that is never good enough for the WBR, who acts as an emotional strip miner.

"How did it make you feel when that man set fire to your house?" the WBR asks, squatting to the level of the dazed and blanketed five-year-old. "I bet it really hurts to watch your house burn to the ground, a nice house like yours. Somebody told me your cat was in that house. That's sad, isn't it? Now you'll never see her again. You'll never see your cat or your shoes or your mother's boyfriend ever again. Can you tell me how that makes you feel inside?"

A PCD was another common icebreaker. Nothing pleases me quite so much as the ever-popular Physically Challenged Detective. Nowhere else on television do you find the blind, deaf, and paralyzed holding down such adventurous and high-paying jobs. Gill once had an idea for a show about a detective in an iron lung called "Last Gasp for Justice." The clients, eager to track down their kidnapped daughter, would gather by the bedside and stroke his forehead, begging him to take the case.

Gill was always full of good ideas. So it shocked me when he changed so suddenly. I never saw it coming. We made plans to meet for dinner at an Indian restaurant that doesn't have a liquor license. You just buy it down the block and carry it in with you — it's cheaper that way. So Gill and I were in the liquor store, where I asked him if we should buy two six-packs and a pint of J&B or one six-pack and a fifth. Or we could just go ahead and get the two six-packs and the fifth because, why not? I was weighing the odds when, out of nowhere, Gill started twisting the buttons on his coat and said, "Forget about me — you just buy something for yourself, Dolph." Dolph is the name I go by because really, nobody can walk around with the name Adolph. It's poison in a name. Dolph is bad too, but it's just box-office poison.

"You go ahead, Dolph. Don't worry about me."

Later in the restaurant, figuring he'd changed his mind, I offered Gill one of my beers. He grew quiet for a few moments, tapping his fork against the table before lowering his head and telling me in fits and starts that he couldn't have anything to drink. "I am, Jesus, Dolph, I am, you know, I'm . . . Well, the thing is that I'm . . . I am an . . . alcoholic."

"Great," I said. "Have eight beers."

Gill became uncharacteristically dramatic, pushing the hair off his forehead. He leaned toward me and said, "I *can't* have a drink, Dolph. Don't you understand anything at all? I *can't.*"

He said it as though he was the recently paralyzed lead dancer in a made-for-TV movie and I had just commanded him to take the lead in tonight's production of *The Nutcracker.* I responded, acting along in what I considered an appropriate manner. "You *can* do it," I said. "I *know* you can do it. But, oh, you'd rather sit there on that chair and be a quitter. Take the easy way out. That's right — you're a loser, a cripple, but when the lights go up on that stage, when all the other dancers are in place, I want you to know the only thing keeping you in that wheelchair is yourself."

Gill's face began to buckle. When he began to sob I realized he wasn't joking. People at the surrounding tables lowered their forks and looked over in our direction. I pointed to our plates and said in a loud whisper, "Whatever you do, don't order the tandoori chicken."

Ever since then things have been different between us. He quit calling me and whenever I called him I got his machine. His old message, the "Broadway doesn't go for pills and booze" line from *Valley of the Dolls,* had been replaced. I know he is home, screening his calls but I always hang up at the point where the new Gill's voice encourages me to take life one day at a time. What has become of him?

I took a train home and talked it over with my mother, who, at the time, was spending a week in the hospital, recovering from surgery to remove cancerous lymph nodes. The cancer was nothing compared to the punishment she endured from her roommate, a lupus patient named Mrs. Gails. The woman never said a word but watched television constantly and at top volume. Possessing no apparent standards she'd watch anything, expressing no more interest in a golf match than a nature program.

"You got any questions about the grazing habits of the adolescent North American bull moose?" my mother asked, fidgeting with the plastic bracelet on her wrist. "I complained to the nurses about the volume but all they do is point to their ears and whisper that she's got a hearing problem. If she's got such a hearing problem then why are they whispering about her? She can hear the food cart from down the hall. I've seen it with my own eyes. She perks up and rubs her hands together and over what? That foraging moose of hers will sit down to a better meal than anything she's likely to get in this place. I want that woman dead."

I talked for a brief while about my problems with Gill until my mother lost interest. "Did I tell you that your sister Charity called me? I hardly recognized her voice because it's been, what, three years since she's phoned me. It seems she lost her job at the suicide hot line and is looking to borrow some money. I said, 'Hold on just a few seconds, darling. It's a bit difficult to reach my purse with this IV in my arm.'"

I listened to her stories with the understanding that the moment my back was turned I would likely become the chief character in her next complaint. I fully expected her to turn to her radiologist and say something like, "Isn't that sweet of my only son to travel all this way so he can whine about his pathetic little friend? Maybe if I weren't strapped to my deathbed I could muster up the strength to give a damn."

That's the sort of thing that destroys my sisters but doesn't bother me in the least. I expect it in a person and am constantly amazed to hear someone refer to it wrongly as gossip and get all bent out of shape about it.

An example: until fairly recently I had the misfortune of holding down a job in the offices of Vincent & Skully Giftware, distributors of needlepoint beer cozies, coffee mugs in the shape of golf bags, and more insipid novelty items than you would ever want to know about.

I equate the decline of this nation with the number of citizens willing to spend money on T-shirts reading "I'm with Stupid," "Retired Prostitute," and "I won't go down in history but I will go down on your little sister." The Vincent & Skully employees were, with the exception of me, perfect reflections of the merchandise. The offices were like a national holding center for the trainably banal, occupied by people who decorated their cubicles with quilted, heart-shaped picture frames and those tiny plush bears with the fierce spring grip that cling to lamps and computer terminals, personalized to read "Terri's bear" or "I wuv you very beary much!"

I don't know how it is that people grow to be so stupid but there is an entire nation of them right outside my door. I lost my job a few months ago when Alisha Cottingham went off the deep end and cornered me in the mail room. Alisha is in the marketing division and she tends to use what she considers to be concise, formal speech. Listening to her speak I imagine she must type it up the night before and commit it all to memory, pacing back and forth in her godforsaken apartment and working to place the perfect emphasis on this or that word.

"Mr. Heck," she began, blocking me off at the Xerox machine. "It has come to my attention here at V&S Giftware that you seem to have some problem with my chin. Now, let me tell you a little something, sir. I am not here to live up to your stringent physical qualifications. I am here to work, as are you. If my chin is, for any reason, keeping you from performing your job here at Vincent & Skully then I believe we have a problem."

I was thinking, chin? What chin? I said something about her neck. Alisha's chins are another story.

She continued. "I just want you to know that your deliberate cruelty cannot hurt me, Mr. Heck, because I will not allow it to. As a professional I am paid to rise above the thoughtless, petty remarks of an office boy who takes pleasure in remarking upon the physical characteristics of his coworkers, many of whom have fought valiantly against both personal and social hardships to make this a company we can all be proud of." Eventually she began to sob and I might have felt sorry for her had she not reported me twice for smoking dope during the three o'clock break. So I made some little remark and it got around. So what? Did Alisha Cottingham honestly believe that by sitting beside me and sharing a bag of potato chips our bond would grow so strong I would fail to notice she has a neck like a stack of dimes?

There seemed to be no stopping her. She finished her speech and started it all over again from the top, each delivery louder until the manager arrived, suggesting I might be happier working somewhere else. Happier?

I called Gill that night to tell him about it. He must have been expecting a call because he answered it on the first ring. Rather than discuss our difficulties I just plowed into the story as if nothing had ever happened. I talked for maybe two minutes tops before he interrupted me to say, "Dolph, I'm sorry but I really don't want to talk to you when you're drunk."

Drunk? I had, you know, some drinks but I wasn't slobbering or anything. I wasn't singing or asking in a weary voice if I will ever find love. I probably couldn't have passed a Breathalyzer test but what does that matter if you're sitting in your own home? It really ticked me off. How come *he* gets to make all the rules? "I'll talk to you when you're sober." So I said, "Yeah, well maybe I'll talk to you when you have red hair and a beard down to your fucking knees."

I had more to say but he hung up before I could complete my thoughts. It bothered the hell out of me, but eventually I came to my senses and realized that sooner or later he's bound to have a relapse. I've read the statistics, and if I know Gill it's just a matter of time before he throws in the towel and starts drinking again. In the meantime I'll just keep my distance.

I had just become comfortable with this prediction when I ran into Gill at a restaurant, and this time I was really drunk. I was at the take-out counter giving my order when I noticed him sitting over a finished meal with three people on the other side of the room. He was wearing a shirt printed with dice, possibly the ugliest shirt I had ever seen on a North American male but still, I was glad to see him. I approached the table and said in a loud voice, "Jesus, Gill, where have you been? Your parole officer has been looking everywhere for you."

Everyone in the restaurant looked up except for Gill, who shook his head and said nothing. Against my better judgment I pulled up a chair and joined their table, introducing myself as an old cellmate from Rikers Island. "Those were the days, weren't they? I think of that bunk bed every day of my life. Remember T-Bone? Remember that guy we all called 'The Rectifier'? Oh, what a time!"

Nobody said anything. Gill rolled his eyes and adjusted the napkin in his lap, which, I assume, sent the "secret coded" message that I was not to be taken seriously. These were the new friends he had met at his meetings, the same type we might have made fun of a few weeks ago. Suddenly, though, they were his people.

A very thin, spent-looking woman with shoulder-length hair gathered in a ponytail cleared her throat and said, "Like I was saying earlier, I thought that Timothy person was very nice. I liked him an awful lot. He's a people person, I could see that right away." This woman was missing one of her front teeth.

Another woman, younger, with heavily moussed blond hair fidgeted with her chopsticks and agreed, saying, "Are you talking about the Timothy with the olive-colored turtleneck and the denim jacket? Oh, I loved that guy. What a nice guy. Was he nice or what?"

"I'd say he's one of the absolute nicest guys I've met in a long time," said the sullen Abe Lincoln lookalike sitting next to me. He paused, scratching at his beard, and small stiff hairs rained onto his empty plate. "I liked Timothy right off the bat because he's just so damned nice how could you not like him?"

"Talk about nice, how about that Chip?" Gill said.

"A chip off the old block," the ugly bearded man said, at which point everyone broke into laughter.

"Ha, ha," I said. "A chip off the old shoulder."

Gill and his companions ignored me until the skinny hag turned to me and said, "You, sir, are standing in the way of our evening and I for one don't appreciate it." I suddenly understood why she was missing her front tooth.

Gill said, "Dolph, maybe you should just try to keep quiet and listen for a change." I nodded and leaned back in my chair, thinking, Listen to what? He's so nice, she's so nice, aren't they so nice. Nice is a mystery to me because while on some mundane level I aspire to it, it is the last thing I would want a table full of dullards saying about me.

"Nice job, Byron."

"Hey, Kimberly, nice blouse. Is it new?"

"I love your haircut, Pepper. It's really nice!"

I don't understand nice. *Nice* is a lazy one-syllable word and it says nothing at all. I prefer to surround myself with more complex words, such as *heroic* and *commanding*.

"That Dolph, is he a national treasure or what?"

I sat at Gill's table for another ten minutes or so during which time I heard the word "nice" twenty-three times until I couldn't stand it anymore. When I finally left, the idiot with the beard called out, "Nice talking to you," which I guess brings the tally up to twenty-four.

I wrote Gill after my mother died, hoping he might pick up the phone and give me a call but instead he chose to mail this hokey calligraphed sympathy card, which I fear he may have actually made himself.

My mother chose to be cremated and the memorial service was sparsely attended — just me, three of my four sisters, my mother's boss from the collection agency, and a few of her acquaintances from the firing range.

During that time at our mother's house my sisters were remote and mechanical, acting as though they were hotel maids, tidying up after a stranger. They spoke as if a terrible chapter of their lives had just ended, and I felt alone in my belief that a much more terrible chapter was about to begin. I overheard them gathered together in the kitchen or talking to their husbands on the telephone, saying, "She was a very sad and angry woman and there's nothing more to say about it." Sad? Maybe.

Angry? Definitely. But there is always more to say about it. My mother made sure of that.

Three days after the memorial service we met with her lawyer, an energetic woman with very long fingernails painted to resemble American flags. Someone, her manicurist I suppose, spent a great deal of time on the stripes but the stars were a mess, a clot of glitter.

She opened her briefcase and informed us that my mother's house, car, and personal possessions were to be sold at their current market value. That money would be added to her life insurance, pension plan, and bank holdings and, according to her will, would be donated to her specified charitable organization, The National Rifle Association.

After the initial shock had worn off, my sisters found themselves plenty more to talk about.

I thought it was funny but, then again, I guess I could afford to think of it as funny. On the afternoon of my last visit, after the radiation and chemotherapy had left her with what would soon become pneumonia, my mother handed me a check for forty thousand dollars and warned me to cash it fast. Mrs. Gails's television was blaring a rerun of a vile situation comedy in which a pleasant-looking, vapid teenaged boy acts as the gamekeeper of four terminally precocious children. "Leave," Mom said, pointing to the door. "And on your way out I want you to shut off her television. It'll take the nurses a good twenty minutes to turn it back on. Give me the gift of peace. It's worth the forty thousand dollars, believe me."

As I left the room she offered to double the money if I smothered Mrs. Gails. "Use the pillow," she called. "The pillow."

I didn't mention the money to my sisters as, like my mother, I may be mean but I'm not stupid. The money has allowed me to take my time and relax a little before stumbling into another meaningless job. I really appreciate it and every afternoon when

I roll out of bed I look up at the asbestos ceiling and silently thank my mother.

For most of my adult life I've held some sort of a regular daytime job so I'm really not used to being at home during a weekday. With all this time on my hands and neither Gill nor my mother to talk to, I find myself watching a great deal of daytime television and drinking much earlier than usual. It had always been my habit to watch television after returning from work. I knew about detectives, lawyers, police dramas, laugh-track comedies, infomercials, movies both good and bad, pageants, commercials, late-night public relations festivals disguised as talk shows, and the valium of anything presented as educational. So it was with great joy that I entered the world of daytime television. Why, I ask, are these programs broadcast when most people are off at work? Daytime TV is a gold mine of pathological behavior.

I move the television from room to room, captivated by just about everything that appears before me. At first I found myself watching with the volume turned to a whisper, lying on the sofa with the TV eight inches from my face. There were times when, in order to reduce the strain on my neck, I actually placed the portable TV on my stomach. I realized later that I'd been thinking about Mrs. Gails. Watching anything at top volume meant that I was, somehow, like her. I pictured my mother's ghost on the other side of my living room, stuffing Kleenex into her ears and calling for the nurse.

"Day and night he's got that TV going. He's brain dead — what more evidence do you need? Pull either his plug or mine because I just can't take it anymore."

All of my neighbors work during the day so little by little I found myself turning up the volume and living a normal television life. I start with what is left of the relentlessly cheerful midmorning advice and interview shows, move through the soap operas, and arrive at the confessional talk shows, which are my favorite. It is their quest for issues that makes these shows irresistible. Recently I watched as a sweatshirt-wearing family appeared to discuss the mother's hiring of a hit man.

"Yes, I set your mattress on fire but only because you bit me on the head."

"I never bit you on your damned head."

"Don't you lie to me. You bit me on the head and I've got the scars to prove it."

"I never bit anyone on the head unless maybe they deserved it because they came home all messed up on needle drugs."

Regardless of the truth I am captured by the story: How could you bite anyone on the head? How could you open your mouth that wide? More interesting are those shows where only one of the guests feels it necessary to state his or her case. I watched a program dedicated to medical mishaps where a denim-clad woman was interviewed alongside her helpless, elderly father. The father, an alcoholic, had received thirty-seven shock treatments following an episode of what his daughter referred to as "Barrel Fever," the D.T.'s. The man sat stooped in a wheelchair, random tufts of dirty white hair clinging to his blistered scalp like lint. He spent a great deal of time clearing his throat and examining a stain on his trousers while his sixty-year-old daughter proudly faced the camera to recall the torment he had visited upon her life. Her father drank and drank until the fever set in, at which point he mistook his wife and children for insects.

"He thought we were bees," the daughter said. "He thought we lived in a hive and came to carry him off to our queen. Remember that?" she asked. "Remember that, Daddy?"

The old man touched his sock and licked his lips. The shock treatments had left him weak and muddled but still his eyes were bright. Whatever his stories he was determined to carry them to his grave in a dignified manner. He remained silent, nodding with pleasure each time his drinking was mentioned.

Given the rarity of truly bizarre acts, the daytime talk shows are forced to pretend that one story is as compelling as the next: the women who have made a lifetime commitment to wearing caftans appearing on Tuesday are equal to the posse of twelve-year-olds who murdered a neighbor's infant son on the grounds that he was ugly. I'd rather hear about the twelve-year-olds and had, in fact, looked forward all day to watching that show when someone dropped by and ruined it for me.

Since losing my job I have become acquainted with my building's super, a pale, burly, red-headed guy by the name of Tommy Keen. He's big all over — tall and wide — dressed in undersized T-shirts that reveal the pasty, sweating flesh of his arms and stomach. Every now and then I'd hear a rap and answer to find Tommy swabbing the tiles outside my apartment, pretending he had knocked accidentally with the mop handle. The guy obviously needed a drink, which was fine by me — I'm not cheap that way. Tommy's problem was that he wasn't content to drink alone. I'd hand the guy a beer and the next thing I knew he'd be hanging out for hours, ruining my afternoon lineup by talking through all my programs. Anything on TV reminded him of a long story revolving around what he referred to as "the women."

"Oh, Dolph," he'd say, watching the paroled rapist face his victim. "The women are going to be the death of me, and you heard it here first."

With Tommy it was never any particular woman but, rather, the entire worldwide lot of them whom he seemed determined to conquer on an intimate basis, one by one, if it took him the rest of his life. I would listen, taking into consideration the fact that you really have to wonder about any male over the age of fifteen who still prefers to go by the name Tommy. I endured him a few afternoons a week until the day I had planned to watch the youth posse, when he actually pounded on my door, begging to be let in. He looked hungover, washed out, more pale than usual, a sweating mess. Tommy brushed past and took a seat on my kitchen table, his hands trembling so bad he could not light his own cigarette.

"So, Tommy," I said, thinking about the program I was certainly going to miss. "So, Tommy, what's shakin'?" He put his doughy head in his hands and kneaded it with his fingers for a few minutes before telling me he'd been having trouble with blackouts.

"Blackouts? What do you mean by that? Was there a power failure in the building that I don't know about?"

Tommy looked at me and shook his head. He released a sigh of hopeless disgust and rose briefly from the chair before settling back down and proceeding to tell me this story: The last thing he remembered it was Sunday evening at around 7:00 P.M. and he was in his living room, having a few drinks and feeding the fish. The next thing he knows it's Wednesday afternoon and he wakes to find himself tied to the radiator with a pair of panty hose. His apartment is completely empty of furniture. He is naked and there are four piles of human shit on the carpet.

Now that's a good story.

We are quiet for a few moments before I say, "Gee, Tommy, it sounds like you've got a real mystery on your hands."

His shoulders began to tremble and I thought, Please don't cry, please, please, please don't cry. He of course began to sob, a painful protracted lowing that, I am fairly certain, stopped in their tracks any species of moose or elk in the surrounding tri-state area. Something told me I should touch him, place my hand on his shoulder but he was my super and he was sweating so I decided to light another cigarette and wait for him to get this out of his system.

He came out of it, finally, choking the words "I . . . just . . . needed to . . . tell . . . somebody and I . . . figured you would . . . understand." His eyes shifted to my trash can, brimming over with empty beer cans and dead bottles of scotch. "I . . . figured you . . . might . . . know where I was . . . coming from."

And that irritated me beyond belief, that he might claim to know me. The last thing I need is a diagnosis from some wasted crybaby who drags a fucking mop for a living. The only reason I ever gave him the time of day was because I felt sorry for him. It ticked me off so I said, "You know, Tommy, I don't quite know how to tell you this but on Tuesday night you came to my door and literally begged me for one hundred dollars."

Tommy lowered his head and shook it slowly from side to side.

"Then you said that if I wouldn't lend the money you'd be willing to earn it the old-fashioned way."

"What's that supposed to mean, 'old-fashioned way'? What are you talking about?"

"Then you sank to your knees and made for my belt buckle."

"No," Tommy moaned, placing his hands over his ears. "That's not possible. You know I'm not that way."

"Well," I said, "you really didn't seem like yourself that night but, then again, I'd never seen you wearing a skirt before. You just seemed so damned desperate that I pulled out my wallet and gave you the hundred dollars."

Tommy rocked back and forth, hugging himself with his freckled arms. "No, God. Oh, please, tell me no." But while Tommy cried "No," some small voice deep inside his tiny brain whispered "Maybe, maybe, maybe."

The following morning I found an envelope containing five twenty-dollar bills slipped beneath my door. Chump. I should have told him five hundred.

A while later I was returning from the Laundromat when I noticed a different guy cleaning the halls. He introduced himself as Eightball and we got to talking. I asked about Tommy and was told that he had checked himself into a rehab center somewhere in New Jersey.

"That Tommy," the new janitor said. "He's a real wild card, isn't he?"

"He sure is, Eightball."

I figure that, wherever he is, Tommy will at least have a good story. If he plays his cards right he'll be wowing them at AA meetings for years to come.

Gill's story, on the other hand, isn't going to impress anyone. I don't even think that being an alcoholic was his idea. It's something he got from his supervisor at work. This guy noticed Gill had been having a couple drinks during his lunch break and called him into the office for a little talk. That night in the Indian restaurant Gill told me how the supervisor had closed the office door and handed him a list of alcoholic warning signs, telling him that he would definitely have to answer "yes" to the question "Does my drinking interfere with my job?" The whole thing was a setup if you ask me. The supervisor spilled out his own story and offered to accompany Gill to a meeting, where, Gill said, "I really started thinking about my life." Then he started magnifying everything, which is a big mistake because if you think too hard about anything it's bound to take the fun out of it. That's what happened to Gill. He's no fun anymore.

I remember saying, "So your boss gave you a quiz — so what? Do you think it's the only quiz in town? I could sit down right now and hand you a pamphlet and say, 'You'll definitely have to answer "yes" to the question "Does my *not* drinking interfere with my friendship with Dolph Heck?"' Take my quiz, why don't you? Why would you listen to some asshole of a supervisor before you'd listen to me? He's just trying to recruit people, that's all. He's a so-called alcoholic so he wants everyone else to be too. Can't you see through that?"

Gill looked at me and said, "I've come to see through a lot of things, Dolph. I've come to see through a lot."

After that there was nothing left to say as nothing gets on my nerves more than someone repeating the same phrase twice. I think it's something people have picked up from television, this emotional stutter. Rather than say something interesting once, they repeat a cliché and hope for the same effect.

Seeing as Gill doesn't have a decent story, I guess he'll be forced to surround himself with people who pride themselves in their ability to understand. It's fine to understand other people but I think it is tiresome to pride yourself in it. Those are the types who will bend over backward to make Gill feel "special," which is sad to me because Gill really is special. I tried to tell him but he wouldn't listen. Actually I probably didn't say *special*, a word that, outside a restaurant, has no value whatsoever. I think I used the term *rare*, another restaurant word.

While Gill is worthy of attention, his story is not. He hasn't even had any blackouts. I've had a few. More than a few, but they always take place in private and they're nothing to write home about, nothing like Tommy's. The closest I've come to the Tommy zone was three weeks ago when I received a telephone bill listing quite a few late-night calls to England. The curious thing is that I do not personally know anyone in England. I thought they'd made a mistake and considered protesting the charges until a few days later when, leafing through a stack of magazines on the living room floor, I came upon a heavily notated page torn from the *TV Guide.* I saw where I had circled and placed seven stars beside that week's three-part PBS "Mystery" presentation. At the bottom of the page were a series of oddly arranged numbers, which looked like locker combinations. These matched the numbers on the phone bill, leading me to assume that I must have actually dialed international information and phoned Scotland Yard at the end of each program to congratulate them on another job well done. Still, though, that's nothing to get worked up about. Exceptional would be to find yourself on a plane headed to England, wearing a tweed cap and demanding that the stewardess put you in touch with Chief Inspector Tennison.

Since receiving my last phone bill I have taken to fastening the telephone to its cradle, using some of the threaded packing tape stolen from what used to be my job. In the rare event of an incoming daytime call I can always grab a knife or scissors, but luckily the task appears to be too strenuous during my ever increasing personal mystery hours. Another problem solved with simplicity and grace.

My next project is to fashion a cushion to the hood of my vacuum cleaner. Again this morning I woke on the kitchen floor with my head resting against the hood of my ancient Hoover.

I ask, "What were you thinking?"

"Mattress, Dolph?"

"Don't go out of your way on my account. I'll just stretch out on this cold tile floor."

"Pillow?"

"No, thanks. This hard plastic vacuum hood will suit me just fine."

This morning, in addition to sleeping on the floor, I awoke to find I had once again wet my pants. It's been happening much more often than is necessary lately and it's beginning to really scare me. This time the urine was induced by a dream in which I had been presented with two citizenship awards, the ceremonies back-to-back. The first award was in the shape of Tommy Keen's head. Made of gold-plated lead it was all I could do to carry it off the stage and into the waiting limo for the next ceremony. It was goofy, the way dreams are. Gill was the limo driver but he didn't seem to remember me. I asked him please to pull over somewhere so I could pee and he kept saying I could use the bathroom at the Pavilion. We argued back and forth until he hit a red light and I jumped out of the limo, leaned against a building, and unzipped my fly. The next thing I knew my face was pressed against the hood of a vacuum cleaner and I was lying in a puddle of urine. I didn't even get to find out what the second prize was. This morning I woke on the kitchen floor in a puddle of urine and understood that something has to change as I am not about to buy rubber sheets or adult diapers. This simply cannot continue.

After my mother's death the most shocking discovery in the box marked "POISON" were not her letters, but the stack of New Year's resolutions she'd spent so long composing. Each of the fifteen cards was dated in the left-hand corner and, in her slanted, childlike writing, each one read the same: "Be good." It shook me up as, in the three years that I myself have been making such lists, mine say the same thing, relatively. I have taken to softening my approach as a safeguard against failure. The last one reads: "Try to think about maybe being good." "Try" and "maybe" give me the confidence I need in order to maintain the casual approach best suited to my ever-changing circumstances.

I looked up at my tightly bound telephone and told myself that I would remain on that floor until someone called, at which point I would answer and redirect my life. Whoever they were and whatever they wanted, I would take it as a sign.

After what seemed like hours, I got off the floor and took a shower, keeping the bathroom door open so I could catch any incoming calls. On the off chance my caller would tell me to quit drinking, I positioned myself on the sofa with two six-packs and a bottle of nice scotch. Then I turned on the TV and ate a sandwich made from leftover chicken lo mein. I call it a Chanwich. At a pivotal point in "One Life to Live" my telephone rang. A woman who introduced herself as Pamela was determined to woo me away from my current long-distance carrier.

"We've been observing your calling patterns, Mr. Heck, and notice that you seem to have several European friends. Did you realize that our company can save you up to twenty-three percent on overseas calls?"

I wound up switching to her company because, seeing as I had made a commitment to change, it seemed cowardly not to honor it. After our conversation I hung up the phone, expecting it to ring again a few minutes later. I thought I was on a roll and that — who knows? — anyone might call, anyone at all.

The phone didn't ring again until sometime around ten in the evening, by which point I was pretty well potted. It was a woman's voice and she started in immediately saying, "All right now, I realize you probably don't remember who I am, do you?" She gave me a moment to guess but I could not begin to identify her.

"It's me, Trudy Chase. I used to be Trudy Cousins. Chase is my married name even though I'm no longer married if *that* makes any sense! Anyway, I don't live in Piedmont anymore but I still have the good old *Post-Democrat* delivered to my door every day and that's where I read the obituary on your mother. I know it's been a while but I just wanted to tell you that I'm very sorry to hear about it."

I didn't know how to respond.

"You really don't remember me, do you?" she said. "It's me, crazy Trudy who used to sit beside you in Mr. Pope's senior English class. Remember me? I was the crazy one. I was the one who wrote 'Don't follow me — I'm lost too' on the back of her graduation gown. It's me, crazy Trudy."

Suddenly I remembered her perfectly. Even at eighteen she struck me as hopeless.

"So, Trudy," I said. "What's going on?"

"Oh, you know me. I'm just as crazy as ever. No, I take that back — I'm probably *crazier* if you can believe that!"

I thought for a moment before saying, "Oh." Because that's really something I can't stand — when people refer to themselves as crazy. The truly crazy are labeled so on the grounds that they see nothing wrong with their behavior. They forge ahead, lighting fires in public buildings and defecating in frying pans without the slightest notion that they are out of step with the rest of society. That, to me, is crazy. Calling yourself crazy is not crazy, only obnoxious.

Trudy went on to tell me that she's lived here in Manhattan for three months, having been transferred from the home office in Piedmont. She chuckled, adding that the people here think she's just about the craziest person they've ever met. She's so crazy that she planned an office party for Lincoln's birthday and petitioned her boss to free the slaves in the accounting department. And she even wore a tall hat and a fake beard! The members of her tenants association thought she should be committed after she hosted the last meeting . . . by candlelight!

"Ha, ha," I said. "That sounds pretty scary."

"Nothing scares me," she said. "That's how crazy I am."

On my silent TV I watched as a defeated wrestler shook his hairbrush at the referee, obviously screaming for a rematch. "Nothing?"

"Not a damned thing," she said. "Nada. Othing nay."

The very idea that, out of nowhere, a member of my 1975 graduating class would call me *and* speak pig latin created a mixed sense of repulsion and endless possibilities.

Trudy spoke of her involvement in any number of organizations. She is, for example, volunteering to walk the dogs of recent stroke victims. "I usually walk with a woman named Marcie, and, Jesus, if you think *I'm* crazy, you should meet her! We call ourselves the Poop Troop, and next week we're getting our uniforms. You should join us sometime."

I pictured myself wearing an "I brake for hydrants" T-shirt and a baseball cap decorated with a synthetic stool.

On top of everything else Trudy also finds the time to play on her company volleyball team, iron for her crazy arthritic neighbor, and teach underprivileged children to make fudge. She didn't say it in a boastful way. She wasn't looking for a medal or trying to make me feel selfish. She invited me over to her apartment for a get-together, but I bowed out, claiming I had a business meeting to attend.

"Well if your meetings are half as crazy as mine you're going to need all the luck you can get," she said.

She asked if she could call me after my meeting and I told her to hold on a moment as I had another call coming in. She's been holding for fifteen minutes now and I still can't make up my mind. I look over at my mother's card on the refrigerator. BE GOOD. But she never specified: Be good to whom? If I'm good to Trudy Chase, I'll tell her never to call me again. If I'm good to myself, I'll wind up making fudge and walking the dogs of stroke victims. Which is worse?

DIARY OF A SMOKER

I RODE my bike to the boat pond in Central Park, where I bought myself a cup of coffee and sat down on a bench to read. I lit a cigarette and was enjoying myself when the woman seated twelve feet away, on the other side of the bench, began waving her hands before her face. I thought she was fighting off a bee.

She fussed at the air and called out, "Excuse me, do you mind if we make this a no-smoking bench?"

I don't know where to begin with a statement like that. "Do you mind if *we* make this a no-smoking bench?" There is no "we." Our votes automatically cancel one another out. What she meant was, "Do you mind if *I* make this a no-smoking bench?" I could understand it if we were in an elevator or locked together in the trunk of a car, but this was outdoors. Who did she think she was? This woman was wearing a pair of sandals, which are always a sure sign of trouble. They looked like the sort of shoes Moses might have worn while he chiseled regulations onto stone tablets. I looked at her sandals and at her rapidly moving arms and I crushed my cigarette. I acted like it was no problem and then I stared at the pages of my book, hating her and Moses — the two of them.

The trouble with aggressive nonsmokers is that they feel they are doing you a favor by not allowing you to smoke. They seem to think that one day you'll look back and thank them for those precious fifteen seconds they just added to your life. What they don't understand is that those are just fifteen more seconds you can spend hating their guts and plotting revenge.

My school insurance expires in a few weeks so I made an appointment for a checkup. It's the only thing they'll pay for as all of my other complaints have been dismissed as "Cosmetic."

If you want a kidney transplant it's covered but if you desperately need a hair transplant it's "Cosmetic." You tell me.

I stood around the examining room for twenty minutes, afraid to poke around as, every so often, a nurse or some confused patient would open the door and wander into the room. And it's bad enough to be caught in your underpants but even worse to be caught in your underpants scratching out a valium prescription on someone else's pad.

When the doctor finally came he looked over my chart and said, "Hey, we have almost the exact same birthday. I'm one day younger than you!"

That did wonders for my morale. It never occurred to me that my doctor could be younger than me. Never entered my mind.

He started in by asking a few preliminary questions and then said, "Do you smoke?"

"Only cigarettes and pot," I answered.

He gave me a look. "*Only* cigarettes and pot? Only?"

"Not crack," I said. "Never touch the stuff. Cigars either. Terrible habit, nasty."

I was at work, defrosting someone's freezer, when I heard the EPA's report on secondhand smoke. It was on the radio and they reported it over and over again. It struck me the same way that previous EPA reports must have struck auto manufacturers and the owners of chemical plants: as reactionary and unfair. The report accuses smokers, especially smoking parents, of criminal recklessness, as if these were people who kept loaded pistols lying on the coffee table, crowded alongside straight razors and mugs of benzene.

Over Christmas we looked through boxes of family pictures and played a game we call "Find Mom, find Mom's cigarettes." There's one in every picture. We've got photos of her pregnant, leaning toward a lit match, and others of her posing with her newborn babies, the smoke forming a halo above our heads. These pictures gave us a warm feeling.

She smoked in the bathtub, where we'd find her drowned butts lined up in a neat row beside the shampoo bottle. She smoked through meals, and often used her half-empty plate as an ashtray. Mom's theory was that if you cooked the meal and did the dishes, you were allowed to use your plate however you liked. It made sense to us.

Even after she was diagnosed with lung cancer she continued to smoke, although less often. On her final trip to the hospital, sick with pneumonia, she told my father she'd left something at home and had him turn the car around. And there, standing at the kitchen counter, she entertained what she knew to be her last cigarette. I hope that she enjoyed it.

It never occurred to any of us that Mom might quit smoking. Picturing her without a cigarette was like trying to imagine her on water skis. Each of us is left to choose our own quality of life and take pleasure where we find it, with the understanding that, like Mom used to say, "Sooner or later, something's going to get you."

Something got me the moment I returned home from work and Hugh delivered his interpretation of the EPA report. He told me that I am no longer allowed to smoke in any room that he currently occupies. Our apartment is small — four tiny rooms.

I told him that seeing as I pay half the rent, I should be allowed to smoke half the time we're in the same room. He agreed, on the condition that every time I light a cigarette, all the windows must be open.

It's cold outside.

GIANTESS

WRITERS! Have fun while earning a few extra bucks writing erotica! *Giantess* magazine needs stories about gals who grow to gigantic proportions! Send sample of work to D.L. Publications."

I circled that ad in this morning's paper and left it lying on my desk while I went to work, staining the bookcases of an art director. This man had, among other artifacts, a pair of delicate porcelain plates, each picturing a single sperm making its reckless journey toward an egg. By mid-afternoon this man had only one such plate. It wasn't necessarily our fault; it just sort of happened. The woman I was working with thought we should leave a confessional note but I thought it might be a better idea to tell him that a squirrel had come in the window, jumped on the dresser, smashed the plate, and left as suddenly as it had arrived. I thought we should scratch the surface of the dresser to suggest destructive claw marks. Lili decided it might be better for her to blame it all on me, seeing as the client was a friend of her brother. That was how we left it.

I came home and wrote a letter to *Giantess* magazine, including a story I had written several years ago. I don't happen to have any giantess stories lying around the house so I sent them something about a short man, hoping they might recognize size as a theme.

I worked today for Marilyn Notkin, stripping the paint off her bedroom windows with a heat gun. I was at it for half an hour when I blew a fuse, at which point I set down my heat gun and headed downstairs to the basement fuse box. On my way back to Marilyn's I popped into the first-floor apartment and joined Kim in watching a few minutes of "Oprah." This morning Oprah's guests were people who had forgiven the unforgivable. One woman had testified on behalf of the man who had stabbed her twenty times. Another had embraced the drunk driver who killed her only son. She invites this fellow over to her house for holidays and Sunday dinners.

"He's like a second son to me now," she said, reaching over to take his hand. "I wouldn't trade Craig for anything." The felon stared at his feet and shrugged his shoulders. I was thinking that a lengthy prison sentence would probably be a lot more comfortable than having to take the place of the person you had killed. I thought it was funny and was laughing when I heard, in the distance, a high-pitched whine like a car alarm but no, not a car alarm. It was shrill and relentless and I was trying to identify it when I remembered the heat gun and ran upstairs to Marilyn's bedroom, where the flaming windowsill had just set fire to the sheer white curtains.

The smoke alarm was screaming and I froze for a moment, watching the curtains change color. And then I was hugging them to my chest and pawing the flames with my hands. I wasn't even thinking, I was so afraid. The fire died in my hands and afterwards, desperately trying to cover my tracks, I wondered what I might say to someone after burning down their house.

"No, I mean it, I'm really, really sorry and just to prove it I'm not going to charge you for today's work. My treat."

The editor of *Giantess* called to say he'd received my letter and thinks I might have potential. He introduced himself as Hank, saying, "I liked your story, Dave, but for *Giantess* you'll need to drop the silly business and get straight to the turn-on if you know what I mean. Do you understand what I'm talking about here, Dave?" Hank told me his readers are interested in women ranging anywhere from ten to seventy-five feet tall and take their greatest delight in the physical description of a giantess outgrowing her clothing. "Do you know what I'm talking about, Dave? I need to *hear* those clothes splitting apart. Do you think you can do that for me?"

It seemed to be something I might be capable of. Hank offered to send me a few back issues and I said it sounded good to me. Later in the afternoon I took a walk to the grocery store, wondering what might cause a woman to grow to such proportions. I think it must be terribly lonely to stand seventy-five feet tall. You'd have no privacy and every bowel movement would evacuate entire cities. What would you eat? A roast chicken would be the size of a peanut. You might put away five dozen but leave with the feeling you were only snacking.

I am working this week on the Upper East Side, assisting a decorative painter named Jeffrey Lee. The clients are renovating their fifteen-room apartment on Fifth Avenue, converting one of the bedrooms into a bathroom for their dogs. I had never in my life witnessed such wealth until this afternoon when Jeffrey and I had lunch in the apartment of the project's interior decorator. I was amazed by the splendor: a Sargent painting in the drawing room, a small Bosch propped up in the kitchen — room after room filled with treasures. The decorator wasn't home so Jeffrey and I had lunch in the kitchen with an estimator and three burly men who had come to replace the dining room windows. I expected that we would sit together and marvel at the grandeur, but instead Jeffrey Lee made a phone call and the men talked shop —window talk, the dullest shoptalk on earth.

"What do you think about those one-and-three-quarter seamless pane liners?" one of the men asked. "I worked with those up on East Eighty-Fourth and, let me tell you, they're a pain in the ass to hoist, but the bastards glaze like you wouldn't believe."

"Hell," another man said, tugging at his T-shirt. "I wouldn't give you two cents for a Champion Eight. I'd rather double-pane three-quarter Stets any day of the week — they're worth two dozen Champions just on installation alone. Double-bind those Stets with a copper-bound Toby Steelhead and you've got yourself a window."

A window washer arrived at the door and the installation foreman pointed to one of his men, saying, "Byron, why don't you take Mr. Clean into the dining room and give him a few pointers on those new Moldonatos?"

The window washer said that he'd been doing his job for thirty-two years and could probably handle it on his own. He wasn't quite ready to start working, so he lit a cigarette and began talking about the recent tragedy involving Eric Clapton's young son, who fell something like fifty floors from his living room window.

"That was over at Seven Fifty-Seven, wasn't it?" the foreman asked.

The window men nodded their heads.

"Seven Fifty-Seven's got those Magnum Double Hungs that start eighteen inches from the floor. Christ, that's low. That Clapton character should have had a goddamned child guard and that's all there is to it!"

The window men agreed.

Then the window washer told a story about a young guy, first day on the job, who fell six stories while washing windows that could have been cleaned from the inside. "This kid didn't know an Acorn Tilt and Turn from a hole in the ground. So he's out there putting his hooks into — get this — the awning rings! Goddamned awning rings couldn't support the weight of a house cat but he digs in and WHAM — falls six floors."

The window men shared a moment of silence.

I asked if the young man died and they all moaned, exhausted by my stupidity.

"Of course he died," the window washer said. "You can't take more than a four-story fall, not in this town anyway."

Then Jeffrey Lee got off the phone and said that, given a choice, he'd rather fall from a higher floor as it would allow more time for his life to flash before his eyes.

The window men said that all depends on the life you led. And then they changed the topic and began discussing women.

In today's mail I received two copies of *Giantess* along with a letter from Hank, who writes, "Please keep in mind that stories featuring continuous, spectacular growth are among the most popular with our readers." The magazines contain stories titled "A Growing Girl," "Blimper," and "The Big Date." There are illustrations and ads for videos, one of which is titled *Trample and Crush.* This is a publication for men who long to explore a vagina the way others might visit the Luray Caverns. Reading it over I noticed that, once they start growing, the women become very moody and aggressive and the knee-high men seem to love it.

My sister once gave me a magazine called *Knocked Up and Gun Toting,* which featured nude, pregnant women sporting firearms: pistols, hunting rifles, Uzis — you name it. I don't imagine *Knocked Up and Gun Toting* has a very wide circulation but I'm certain its subscribers are devoted and happy in their own way. Still, though, like with *Giantess,* I have a hard time sharing their fetish. I shudder at the thought of nipples the size of manhole covers. Beneath the surface the *Giantess* reader seems to be a man who longs for his infancy. He looks back fondly at the time he was dwarfed by his mother and scolded for soiling himself. And that's just about the last experience I care to reflect upon. Sure I received a few spankings but I never considered them a high point. I moved ahead and got on with my life. Didn't I?

THE CURLY KIND

I WAS carrying out the Rosenblatt's garbage this afternoon when the maid from the next apartment closed the door behind her, straightened her white uniform, and pushed the button for the elevator. This is the twelfth floor, four apartments per level and only one elevator, so it usually takes a while. I watched as the maid was joined by two young children accompanied by an Irish nanny. As they waited, the nanny reached into her canvas bag and handed the boy a bag of Cheetos, which he opened and immediately emptied onto the floor, screaming, "I wanted the CURLY kind. Don't you know ANYTHING?"

The nanny lowered her head while the maid and I locked eyes and shrugged our shoulders as if to say, "What can you do?" The elevator arrived and they boarded, leaving behind an orange mat of uncurly Cheetos, which will be crushed by the twelfth-floor tenants until a janitor is dispatched to sweep them up.

I have seen this next-door maid three or four times before. She is a refrigerator-sized dark-skinned woman wearing loafers with the backs cut away to make them more comfortable. I see her and think of Lena Payne.

My mother was never much of a housekeeper and it drove me to distraction, the chaos of our home. Five years after moving to Raleigh we still had Mayflower boxes in the living room. I would return home from school, place my coat and books neatly in my bedroom, activate the vacuum cleaner and set to work gathering my sisters' clothing, their half-empty glasses, and the bowls of potato chip crumbs left before the television set, washing dishes, polishing furniture, and thinking that *it wasn't fair.* I had been switched at birth and carried back to the wrong household. Somewhere my natural family spent their days observing strict laboratory conditions, wondering what had become of me. My own bedroom was immaculate, a shrine. I cleaned it every day. My sisters were not allowed to cross the threshold. They stood in the hallway, observing me as if I were an exotic zoo animal displayed in his natural habitat.

While my mother was pregnant with her sixth child, my father finally gave in and allowed her to hire a housekeeper one day a week. When Lena was introduced I thought that finally we were getting somewhere. I left for school as my mother turned on the portable TV and handed her a cup of coffee. I returned from school seven hours later to find an ironing board in the kitchen, Mom and Lena in roughly the same position — watching TV and drinking coffee.

It struck me as the perfect union: the two laziest people on the face of the earth coming together to watch "Mike Douglas" and "General Hospital." I ran to touch the vacuum cleaner and found it stone cold. It wasn't fair.

Normally Mom would drive Lena to the shopping center,

where she caught a ride home with a friend, but one day there was something good on TV so Lena stayed late. My mother offered to take her home, and I went along for the ride. We drove past the Raleigh I knew, beyond the paved streets and onto narrow dirt roads lined with shacks — actual shacks, the type I had seen in *Life* magazine. When our station wagon pulled up, Lena's shack emptied and seven children gathered on the porch, shielding their eyes with their hands. The yard was bald and dusty, populated with chickens. I had never before seen a live chicken and decided I would like to have one as a pet. Lena said that I could have one if I could catch it. Identifying the chicken of my choice I immediately pictured her living in my own grassy yard, prancing for grain. Her name would be Penny, and every day she would kneel down and thank God that she lived with me and not with Lena. I thought that this chicken might come to me if I spoke to her in a comforting voice. I thought you could convince a chicken with the promise of a better life. When that didn't work I decided I might tackle a chicken and I tried, again and again. I dove for her, soiling my school clothes in clouds of dirt and dust. Finally I gave up. Standing to wipe the clay off my face I turned to see everyone laughing at me: Lena, her seven children, even my own mother doubled over in the front seat of the car. I remember turning toward the shack yelling, "I don't need your filthy chickens. We buy our own — from the store."

In the car on the way home my mother tried in vain to convey the shame I had brought against her but I wasn't listening. My only response was to swear off chicken for the next few weeks. Whenever one was served I pictured the steaming carcass raising a cartoon head and laughing at me. It was years before I thought of things differently.

This afternoon I went to G.L.'s apartment to clean his venetian blinds, which had been soiled during a fire. I first met this man last week when I was sent to unpack his books and arrange them on the shelves in alphabetical order. He's got quite a library:

leather-bound editions of Jane Austen and Émile Zola sandwiching several cookbooks and countless manuals devoted to the study of sadomasochistic sex. This morning G.L. answered the door in his bathrobe, drinking black coffee from a mug shaped to resemble a boot. He is not a pleasant man but seems to get along fine in the world as long as he has his way. He led me to the nearest window and suggested I use Formula 409 and paper towel, but that would have taken me weeks. Having experience with blinds I thought it might be quicker and more productive if I took them down and washed them in the tub. I thought he would argue with me but instead he took off his bathrobe saying, "Sure, whatever." He stood for a moment in his underpants before walking into the bathroom, where he ran water into the sink, preparing to shave something. G.L.'s bathroom is tiny and I thought he might need some privacy, so I just sort of stood around the living room until he called out, "Hey, are you going to clean those blinds or not? I'm not made of money."

I took down one of the blinds, slowly and carefully as if I were removing a tumor from a sensitive area of the brain. I stood with the blinds in my hands and counted to twenty. Then to thirty. He called out again and I had no choice but to press against him as I entered the bathroom. I passed him at the sink and made my way to the tub, where I knelt down and commenced to bathe the venetian blinds in water and ammonia. G.L. had a television propped beside the sink, a portable TV the size of a car battery, which he would constantly curse and rechannel. I couldn't see the screen but listened as he groused his way from one Saturday-afternoon program to another before settling on an infomercial devoted to something called "The Oxygen Cocktail." From what I could hear I gathered that The Oxygen Cocktail is some sort of a pick-me-up made from clarified air. The commercial suggested that early cavemen enjoyed a highly satisfying oxygen content, which afforded them the stamina to produce magnificent cave paintings and still find the energy to hunt mastadons. Participants in the recent Olympic Games testified to the virtues of The Oxygen Cocktail, and I listened while bending over the bathtub, scrubbing a sadist's blinds with ammonia. I wanted to part the shower curtain, curious to see this Oxygen Cocktail. Does it come in a can, a bottle, a nasal spray? Were the Olympians in swimsuits or street clothes?

The blinds weren't coming clean the way I'd hoped so I added some Clorox to the mixture, a stupid thing to do. The combination of ammonia and chloride can be lethal but I've discovered it can work miracles as long as you keep telling yourself, "I want to live, I want to live. . . ." I tried reminding myself of that fact. I pictured myself finishing the job and returning home to a refreshing Oxygen Cocktail. My throat began to burn and I heard G.L. begin to buckle and cough. When he parted the curtain asking, "Are you trying to kill me?" I had to think hard for the answer.

Bart and I cleaned the apartment of another "Sesame Street" writer — that's the third one this month. I've never met any of these people but each of them has a little shrine where they display plush models of Grover and Big Bird along with eight Emmy Awards won for children's television. Eight of them. I had never seen an Emmy in person and noticed how the styles have changed over the years. This afternoon's writer had her awards marching in a neat row along the window ledge. It made me sad to see how a few of the earlier models had corroded. I had always imagined them to be made of pure gold but they're plated. Still, though, they have a satisfying weight, a heaviness that suggests achievement. I lifted each award in order to clean the window ledge and, as long as I had it in my hands, I posed before the full-length mirror, looking humble.

"I really wasn't prepared for this," I said, hoping the audience might believe me. I have spent the better part of my life planning my awards speeches and always begin with that line. It is tiresome to listen as winners thank people most of us have never heard of, but in my award fantasies I like to mention everyone from my twelfth-grade English teacher to the Korean market where I buy my cigarettes and cat food. And that's what's nice about eight Emmys. Lifting each one I addressed the mirror, saying, "But most of all I'd like to thank Amy, Lisa, Gretchen, Paul, Sharon, Lou, and Tiffany for their support." Then I picked up the next, moving on to Hugh, Evelyne, Ira, Susan, Jim, Ronnie, Marge, and Steve. By my eighth Emmy I was groping for names. I was standing there, trying to remember the name of a counselor from Camp Cheerio when Bart entered the room and I realized with shame that I had forgotten to thank him.

SANTALAND DIARIES

I WAS in a coffee shop looking through the want ads when I read, "Macy's Herald Square, the largest store in the world, has big opportunities for outgoing, fun-loving people of all shapes and sizes who want more than just a holiday job! Working as an elf in Macy's SantaLand means being at the center of the excitement. . . ."

I circled the ad and then I laughed out loud at the thought of it. The man seated next to me turned on his stool, checking to see if I was a lunatic. I continued to laugh, quietly. Yesterday I applied for a job at UPS. They are hiring drivers' helpers for the upcoming Christmas season and I went to their headquarters filled with hope. In line with three hundred other men and women my hope diminished. During the brief interview I was asked why I wanted to work for UPS and I answered that I wanted to work for UPS because I like the brown uniforms. What did they expect me to say?

"I'd like to work for UPS because, in my opinion, it's an opportunity to showcase my substantial leadership skills in one of the finest private delivery companies this country has seen since the Pony Express!"

I said I liked the uniforms and the UPS interviewer turned my application facedown on his desk and said, "Give me a break."

I came home this afternoon and checked the machine for a message from UPS but the only message I got was from the company that holds my student loan, Sallie Mae. Sallie Mae sounds like a naive and barefoot hillbilly girl but in fact they are a ruthless and aggressive conglomeration of bullies located in a tall brick building somewhere in Kansas. I picture it to be the tallest building in that state and I have decided they hire their employees straight out of prison. It scares me.

The woman at Macy's asked, "Would you be interested in full-time elf or evening and weekend elf?"

I said, "Full-time elf."

I have an appointment next Wednesday at noon.

I am a thirty-three-year-old man applying for a job as an elf.

I often see people on the streets dressed as objects and handing out leaflets. I tend to avoid leaflets but it breaks my heart to see a grown man dressed as a taco. So, if there is a costume involved, I tend not only to accept the leaflet, but to accept it graciously, saying, "Thank you so much," and thinking, "You poor, pathetic son of a bitch. I don't know what you have but I hope I never catch it." This afternoon on Lexington Avenue I accepted a leaflet from a man dressed as a camcorder. Hot dogs, peanuts, tacos, video cameras, these things make me sad because they don't fit in on the streets. In a parade, maybe, but not on the streets. I figure that at least as an elf I will have a place; I'll be in Santa's Village with all the other elves. We will reside in a fluffy wonderland surrounded by candy canes and gingerbread shacks. It won't be quite as sad as standing on some street corner dressed as a french fry.

I am trying to look on the bright side. I arrived in New York three weeks ago with high hopes, hopes that have been challenged. In my imagination I'd go straight from Penn Station to the offices of "One Life to Live," where I would drop off my bags and spruce up before heading off for drinks with Cord Roberts and Victoria Buchannon, the show's greatest stars. We'd sit in a plush booth at a tony cocktail lounge where my new celebrity friends would lift their frosty glasses in my direction and say, "A toast to David Sedaris, the best writer this show has ever had!!!"

I'd say, "You guys, cut it out." It was my plan to act modest.

People at surrounding tables would stare at us, whispering, "Isn't that . . . ? Isn't that . . . ?"

I might be distracted by their enthusiasm and Victoria Buchannon would lay her hand over mine and tell me that I'd better get used to being the center of attention.

But instead I am applying for a job as an elf. Even worse than applying is the very real possibility that I will not be hired, that I couldn't even find work as an elf. That's when you know you're a failure.

This afternoon I sat in the eighth-floor SantaLand office and was told, "Congratulations, Mr. Sedaris. You are an elf."

In order to become an elf I filled out ten pages' worth of forms, took a multiple choice personality test, underwent two interviews, and submitted urine for a drug test. The first interview was general, designed to eliminate the obvious sociopaths. During the second interview we were asked why we wanted to be elves. This is always a problem question. I listened as the woman ahead of me, a former waitress, answered the question, saying, "I really want to be an elf? Because I think it's about acting? And before this I worked in a restaurant? Which was run by this really wonderful woman who had a dream to open a restaurant? And it made me realize that it's really really . . . important to have a . . . dream?"

Everything this woman said, every phrase and sentence, was punctuated with a question mark and the interviewer never raised an eyebrow.

When it was my turn I explained that I wanted to be an elf because it was one of the most frightening career opportunities I had ever come across. The interviewer raised her face from my application and said, "And . . . ?"

I'm certain that I failed my drug test. My urine had roaches and stems floating in it, but still they hired me because I am short, five feet five inches. Almost everyone they hired is short. One is a dwarf. After the second interview I was brought to the manager's office, where I was shown a floor plan. On a busy day twenty-two thousand people come to visit Santa, and I was told that it is an elf's lot to remain merry in the face of torment and adversity. I promised to keep that in mind.

I spent my eight-hour day with fifty elves and one perky, well-meaning instructor in an enormous Macy's classroom, the walls of which were lined with NCR 2152's. A 2152, I have come to understand, is a cash register. The class was broken up into study groups and given assignments. My group included several returning elves and a few experienced cashiers who tried helping me by saying things like, "Don't you even know your personal ID code? Jesus, I had mine memorized by ten o'clock."

Everything about the cash register intimidates me. Each procedure involves a series of codes: separate numbers for cash, checks, and each type of credit card. The term *Void* has gained prominence as the filthiest four-letter word in my vocabulary. Voids are a nightmare of paperwork and coded numbers, everything produced in triplicate and initialed by the employee and his supervisor.

Leaving the building tonight I could not shake the mental picture of myself being stoned to death by restless, angry customers, their nerves shattered by my complete lack of skill. I tell myself that I will simply pry open my register and accept anything they want to give me — beads, cash, watches, whatever. I'll negotiate and swap. I'll stomp their credit cards through the masher, write "Nice Knowing You!" along the bottom of the slip and leave it at that.

All we sell in SantaLand are photos. People sit upon Santa's lap and pose for a picture. The Photo Elf hands them a slip of paper with a number printed along the top. The form is filled out by another elf and the picture arrives by mail weeks later. So really, all we sell is the idea of a picture. One idea costs nine dollars, three ideas cost eighteen.

My worst nightmare involves twenty-two thousand people a day standing before my register. I won't always be a cashier, just once in a while. The worst part is that after I have accumulated three hundred dollars I have to remove two hundred, fill out half a dozen forms, and run the envelope of cash to the drop in the China Department or to the vault on the balcony above the first floor. I am not allowed to change my clothes beforehand. I have to go dressed as an elf. An elf in SantaLand is one thing, an elf in Sportswear is something else altogether.

This afternoon we were given presentations and speeches in a windowless conference room crowded with desks and plastic chairs. We were told that during the second week of December, SantaLand is host to "Operation Special Children," at which time poor children receive free gifts donated by the store. There is another morning set aside for terribly sick and deformed children. On that day it is an elf's job to greet the child at the Magic Tree and jog back to the house to brace our Santa.

"The next one is missing a nose," or "Crystal has third-degree burns covering 90 percent of her body."

Missing a nose. With these children Santa has to be careful not to ask, "And what would *you* like for Christmas?"

We were given a lecture by the chief of security, who told us that Macy's Herald Square suffers millions of dollars' worth of employee theft per year. As a result the store treats its employees the way one might treat a felon with a long criminal record. Cash rewards are offered for turning people in and our bags are searched every time we leave the store. We were shown videotapes in which supposed former employees hang their heads and rue the day they ever thought to steal that leather jacket. The actors faced the camera to explain how their arrests had ruined their friendships, family life, and, ultimately, their future.

One fellow stared at his hands and sighed, "There's no way I'm going to be admitted into law school. Not now. Not after what I've done. Nope, no way." He paused and shook his head of the unpleasant memory. "Oh, man, not after this. No way."

A lonely, reflective girl sat in a coffee shop, considered her empty cup, and moaned, "I remember going out after work with all my Macy's friends. God, those were good times. I loved those people." She stared off into space for a few moments before continuing, "Well, needless to say, those friends aren't calling anymore. This time I've *really* messed up. Why did I do it? Why?"

Macy's has two jail cells on the balcony floor and it apprehends three thousand shoplifters a year. We were told to keep an eye out for pickpockets in SantaLand.

Interpreters for the deaf came and taught us to sign "MERRY CHRISTMAS! I AM SANTA'S HELPER." They told us to speak as we sign and to use bold, clear voices and bright facial expressions. They taught us to say "YOU ARE A VERY PRETTY BOY/GIRL! I LOVE YOU! DO YOU WANT A SURPRISE?"

My sister Amy lives above a deaf girl and has learned quite a bit of sign language. She taught some to me and so now I am able to say, "SANTA HAS A TUMOR IN HIS HEAD THE SIZE OF AN OLIVE. MAYBE IT WILL GO AWAY TOMORROW BUT I DON'T THINK SO."

This morning we were lectured by the SantaLand managers and presented with a Xeroxed booklet of regulations titled "The

Elfin Guide." Most of the managers are former elves who have worked their way up the candy-cane ladder but retain vivid memories of their days in uniform. They closed the meeting saying, "I want you to remember that even if you are assigned Photo Elf on a busy weekend, YOU ARE NOT SANTA'S SLAVE."

In the afternoon we were given a tour of SantaLand, which really is something. It's beautiful, a real wonderland, with ten thousand sparkling lights, false snow, train sets, bridges, decorated trees, mechanical penguins and bears, and really tall candy canes. One enters and travels through a maze, a path which takes you from one festive environment to another. The path ends at the Magic Tree. The Tree is supposed to resemble a complex system of roots, but looks instead like a scale model of the human intestinal tract. Once you pass the Magic Tree, the light dims and an elf guides you to Santa's house. The houses are cozy and intimate, laden with toys. You exit Santa's house and are met with a line of cash registers.

We traveled the path a second time and were given the code names for various posts, such as "The Vomit Corner," a mirrored wall near the Magic Tree, where nauseous children tend to surrender the contents of their stomachs. When someone vomits, the nearest elf is supposed to yell "VAMOOSE," which is the name of the janitorial product used by the store. We were taken to the "Oh, My God, Corner," a position near the escalator. People arriving see the long line and say "Oh, my God!" and it is an elf's job to calm them down and explain that it will take no longer than an hour to see Santa.

On any given day you can be an Entrance Elf, a Water Cooler Elf, a Bridge Elf, Train Elf, Maze Elf, Island Elf, Magic Window Elf, Emergency Exit Elf, Counter Elf, Magic Tree Elf, Pointer Elf, Santa Elf, Photo Elf, Usher Elf, Cash Register Elf, Runner Elf, or Exit Elf. We were given a demonstration of the various positions in action, performed by returning elves who were so animated and relentlessly cheerful that it embarrassed me to walk past them. I don't know that I could look someone in the eye and exclaim, "Oh, my goodness, I think I see Santa!" or "Can you close your eyes and make a very special Christmas wish!" Everything these elves said had an exclamation point at the end of it!!! It makes one's mouth hurt to speak with such forced merriment. I feel cornered when someone talks to me this way. Doesn't everyone? I prefer being frank with children. I'm more likely to say, "You must be exhausted," or "I know a lot of people who would kill for that little waistline of yours."

I am afraid I won't be able to provide the grinding enthusiasm Santa is asking for. I think I'll be a low-key sort of an elf.

Today was elf dress rehearsal. The lockers and dressing rooms are located on the eighth floor, directly behind SantaLand. Elves have gotten to know one another over the past four days of training but once we took off our clothes and put on the uniforms everything changed.

The woman in charge of costuming assigned us our outfits and gave us a lecture on keeping things clean. She held up a calendar and said, "Ladies, you know what this is. Use it. I have scraped enough blood out from the crotches of elf knickers to last me the rest of my life. And don't tell me, 'I don't wear underpants, I'm a dancer.' You're not a dancer. If you were a real dancer you wouldn't be here. You're an elf and you're going to wear panties like an elf."

My costume is green. I wear green velvet knickers, a yellow turtleneck, a forest-green velvet smock, and a perky stocking cap decorated with spangles. This is my work uniform.

My elf name is Crumpet. We were allowed to choose our own names and given permission to change them according to our outlook on the snowy world.

Today was the official opening day of SantaLand and I worked as a Magic Window Elf, a Santa Elf, and an Usher Elf. The Magic Window is located in the adult "Quick Peep" line. My job was to say, "Step on the Magic Star and look through the window, and you can see Santa!" I was at the Magic Window for fifteen minutes before a man approached me and said, "You look so fucking stupid."

I have to admit that he had a point. But still, I wanted to say that at least I get paid to look stupid, that he gives it away for free. But I can't say things like that because I'm supposed to be merry.

So instead I said, "Thank you!"

"Thank you!" as if I had misunderstood and thought he had said, "You look terrific."

"Thank you!"

He was a brawny wise guy wearing a vinyl jacket and carrying a bag from Radio Shack. I should have said, real loud, "Sorry man, I don't date other guys."

Two New Jersey families came together to see Santa. Two loud, ugly husbands with two wives and four children between them. The children gathered around Santa and had their picture taken. When Santa asked the ten-year-old boy what he wanted for Christmas, his father shouted, "A WOMAN! GET HIM A WOMAN, SANTA!" These men were very loud and irritating, constantly laughing and jostling one another. The two women sat on Santa's lap and had their pictures taken and each asked Santa for a Kitchen-Aide brand dishwasher and a decent winter coat. Then the husbands sat on Santa's lap and, when asked what he wanted for Christmas, one of the men yelled, "I WANT A BROAD WITH BIG TITS." The man's small-breasted wife crossed her arms over her chest, looked at the floor, and gritted her teeth. The man's son tried to laugh.

Again this morning I got stuck at the Magic Window, which is really boring. I'm supposed to stand around and say, "Step on the Magic Star and you can see Santa!" I said that for a while and then I started saying, "Step on the Magic Star and you can see Cher!"

And people got excited. So I said, "Step on the Magic Star and you can see Mike Tyson!"

Some people in the other line, the line to sit on Santa's lap, got excited and cut through the gates so that they could stand on my Magic Star. Then they got angry when they looked through the Magic Window and saw Santa rather than Cher or Mike Tyson. What did they honestly expect? Is Cher so hard up for money that she'd agree to stand behind a two-way mirror at Macy's?

The angry people must have said something to management because I was taken off the Magic Star and sent to Elf Island, which is really boring as all you do is stand around and act merry. At noon a huge group of retarded people came to visit Santa and passed me on my little island. These people were profoundly retarded. They were rolling their eyes and wagging their tongues and staggering toward Santa. It was a large group of retarded people and after watching them for a few minutes I could not begin to guess where the retarded people ended and the regular New Yorkers began.

Everyone looks retarded once you set your mind to it.

This evening I was sent to be a Photo Elf, a job I enjoyed the first few times. The camera is hidden in the fireplace and I take the picture by pressing a button at the end of a cord. The pictures arrive by mail weeks later and there is no way an elf can be identified and held accountable but still, you want to make it a good picture.

During our training we were shown photographs that had gone wrong, blurred frenzies of an elf's waving arm, a picture blocked by a stuffed animal, the yawning Santa. After every photograph an elf must remove the numbered form that appears at the bottom of the picture. A lazy or stupid elf could ruin an entire roll of film, causing eager families to pay for and later receive photographs of complete, beaming strangers.

Taking someone's picture tells you an awful lot, *awful* being the operative word. Having the parents in the room tends to make it even worse. It is the SantaLand policy to take a picture of every child, which the parent can either order or refuse. People are allowed to bring their own cameras, video recorders, whatever. It is the multimedia groups that exhaust me. These are parents bent over with equipment, relentless in their quest for documentation.

I see them in the Maze with their video cameras instructing their children to act surprised. "Monica, baby, look at the train set and then look back at me. No, look at *me.* Now wave. That's right, wave hard."

The parents hold up the line and it is a Maze Elf's job to hurry them along.

"Excuse me, sir, I'm sorry but we're sort of busy today and I'd appreciate it if you could maybe wrap this up. There are quite a few people behind you."

The parent then asks you to stand beside the child and wave. I do so. I stand beside a child and wave to the video camera, wondering where I will wind up. I picture myself on the television set in a paneled room in Wapahanset or Easternmost Meadows. I picture the family fighting over command of the remote control, hitting the fast-forward button. The child's wave becomes a rapid salute. I enter the picture and everyone in the room entertains the same thought: "What's that asshole doing on our Christmas Memory tape?"

The moment these people are waiting for is the encounter with Santa. As a Photo Elf I watch them enter the room and take control.

"All right, Ellen, I want you and Marcus to stand in front of Santa and when I say, 'now,' I want you to get onto his lap. Look at me. Look at Daddy until I tell you to look at Santa."

He will address his wife who is working the still camera and she will crouch low to the ground with her light meter and a Nikon with many attachments. It is heavy and the veins in her arms stand out.

Then there are the multimedia families in groups, who say,

"All right, now let's get a shot of Anthony, Damascus, Theresa, Doug, Amy, Paul, *and* Vanity — can we squeeze them all together? Santa, how about you let Doug sit on your shoulders, can we do that?"

During these visits the children are rarely allowed to discuss their desires with Santa. They are too busy being art-directed by the parents.

"Vanity and Damascus, look over here, no, look *here.*"

"Santa, can you put your arm around Amy and shake hands with Paul at the same time?"

"That's good. That's nice."

I have seen parents sit their child upon Santa's lap and immediately proceed to groom: combing hair, arranging a hemline, straightening a necktie. I saw a parent spray their child's hair, Santa treated as though he were a false prop made of cement, turning his head and wincing as the hair spray stung his eyes.

Young children, ages two to four, tend to be frightened of Santa. They have no interest in having their pictures taken because they don't know what a picture is. They're not vain, they're babies. They are babies and they act accordingly — they cry. A Photo Elf understands that, once a child starts crying, it's over. They start crying in Santa's house and they don't stop until they are at least ten blocks away.

When the child starts crying, Santa will offer comfort for a moment or two before saying, "Maybe we'll try again next year."

The parents had planned to send the photos to relatives and place them in scrapbooks. They waited in line for over an hour and are not about to give up so easily. Tonight I saw a woman slap and shake her sobbing daughter, yelling, "Goddamn it, Rachel, get on that man's lap and smile or I'll give you something to cry about."

I often take photographs of crying children. Even more grotesque is taking a picture of a crying child with a false grimace. It's not a smile so much as the forced shape of a smile. Oddly, it pleases the parents.

"Good girl, Rachel. Now, let's get the hell out of here. Your mother has a headache that won't quit until you're twenty-one."

At least a third of Santa's visitors are adults: couples, and a surprising number of men and women alone. Most of the single people don't want to sit on Santa's lap; they just stop by to shake his hand and wish him luck. Often the single adults are foreigners who just happened to be shopping at Macy's and got bullied into the Maze by the Entrance Elf, whose job it is to hustle people in. One moment the foreigner is looking at china, and the next thing he knows he is standing at the Magic Tree, where an elf holding a palm-sized counter is asking how many in his party are here to see Santa.

"How many in your party?"

The foreigner answers, "Yes."

"How many in your party is not a yes or no question."

"Yes."

Then a Santa Elf leads the way to a house where the confused and exhausted visitor addresses a bearded man in a red suit, and says, "Yes, OK. Today I am good." He shakes Santa's hand and runs, shaken, for the back door.

This afternoon a man came to visit Santa, a sloppy, good-looking man in his mid-forties. I thought he was another confused European, so I reassured him that many adults come to visit Santa, everyone is welcome. An hour later, I noticed the same man, back again to fellowship with Santa. I asked what he and Santa talk about, and in a cracked and puny voice he answered, "Toys. All the toys."

I noticed a dent in the left side of his forehead. You could place an acorn in a dent like this. He waited in line and returned to visit a third time. On his final visit he got so excited he peed on Santa's lap.

So far in SantaLand, I have seen Simone from "General Hospital," Shawn from "All My Children," Walter Cronkite, and Phil Collins. Last year one of the elves was suspended after asking Goldie Hawn to autograph her hand. We have been instructed to leave the stars alone.

Walter Cronkite was very tall, and I probably wouldn't have recognized him unless someone had pointed him out to me. Phil Collins was small and well groomed. He arrived with his daughter and an entourage of three. I don't care about Phil Collins one way or the other but I saw some people who might and I felt it was my duty to tap them on the shoulder and say, "Look, there's Phil Collins!"

Many of Santa's visitors are from out of town and welcome the opportunity to view a celebrity, as it rounds out their New York experience. I'd point out Phil Collins and people would literally squeal with delight. Seeing as it is my job to make people happy, I didn't have any problem with it. Phil Collins wandered through the Maze, videotaping everything with his camcorder and enjoying himself. Once he entered the Magic Tree, he was no longer visible to the Maze audience, so I began telling people that if they left immediately and took a right at the end of the hall, they could probably catch up with Phil Collins after his visit with Santa. So they did. People left. When Phil Collins walked out of SantaLand, there was a crowd of twenty people waiting for autographs. When the managers came looking for the big mouth, I said, "Phil Collins, who's he?"

I spent a few hours in the Maze with Puff, a young elf from Brooklyn. We were standing near the Lollipop Forest when we realized that *Santa* is an anagram of *Satan.* Father Christmas or the Devil — so close but yet so far. We imagined a SatanLand where visitors would wade through steaming pools of human blood and feces before arriving at the Gates of Hell, where a hideous imp in a singed velvet costume would take them by the hand and lead them toward Satan. Once we thought of it we couldn't get it out of our minds. Overhearing the customers we would substitute the word *Satan* for the word *Santa.*

"What do you think, Michael? Do you think Macy's has the real Satan?"

"Don't forget to thank Satan for the Baby Alive he gave you last year."

"I love Satan."

"Who doesn't? Everyone loves Satan."

I would rather drive upholstery tacks into my gums than work as the Usher Elf. The Usher stands outside Santa's exit door and fills out the photo forms. While I enjoy trying to guess where people are from, I hate listening to couples bicker over how many copies they want.

It was interesting the first time I did it, but not anymore. While the parents make up their minds, the Usher has to prevent the excited children from entering Santa's back door to call out the names of three or four toys they had neglected to request earlier.

When things are slow, an Usher pokes in his head and watches Santa with his visitors. This afternoon we were slow and I watched a forty-year-old woman and her ancient mother step in to converse with Santa. The daughter wore a short pink dress, decorated with lace — the type of dress that a child might wear. Her hair was trained into pigtails and she wore ruffled socks and patent leather shoes. This forty-year-old girl ran to Santa and embraced him, driving rouge into his beard. She spoke in a baby voice and then lowered it to a whisper. When they left I asked if they wanted to purchase the photo and the biggest little girl in the world whispered something in her mother's ear and then she skipped away. She skipped. I watched her try and commune with the youngsters standing around the register until her mother pulled her away.

This morning I spent some time at the Magic Window with Sleighbell, an entertainer who is in the process of making a music video with her all-girl singing group. We talked about one thing and another, and she told me that she has appeared on a few television shows, mainly soap operas. I asked if she has ever done "One Life to Live," and she said, yes, she had a bit part as a flamenco dancer a few years ago when Cord and Tina remarried and traveled to Madrid for their honeymoon.

Suddenly I remembered Sleighbell perfectly. On that episode she wore a red lace dress and stomped upon a shiny nightclub floor until Spain's greatest bullfighter entered, challenging Cord to a duel. Sleighbell intervened. She stopped dancing and said to Cord, "Don't do it, Señor. Yoot be a fool to fight weeth Spain's greatest boolfighter!"

Sleighbell told me that the honeymoon was filmed here in the New York studio. That surprised me as I really thought it was shot in Spain. She told me that the dancing scene was shot in the late morning and afterwards there was a break for lunch. She took her lunch in the studio cafeteria and was holding her tray, when Tina waved her over to her table. Sleighbell had lunch with Tina! She said that Tina was very sweet and talked about her love for Smokey Robinson. I had read that Tina had driven a wedge between Smokey and his wife, but it was thrilling to hear it from someone who had the facts.

Later in the day I was put on the cash register where Andrea, one of the managers, told me that her friend Caroline was the person responsible for casting on "One Life to Live." It was Caroline who replaced the old Tina with the new Tina. I loved the old Tina and will accept no substitutes, but I told Andrea that I liked the new Tina a lot, and she said, "I'll pass that along to Caroline. She'll be happy to hear it!" We were talking when Mitchell, another manager, got involved and said that he'd been on "One Life to Live" seven times. He played Clint's lawyer five years ago when the entire Buchannon family was on trial for the murder of Mitch Laurence. Mitchell knows Victoria Buchannon personally and said that she's just as sweet and caring in real life as she is on the show.

"She's basically playing herself, except for the multiple personality disorder," he said, pausing to verify a check on another elf's register. He asked the customer for another form of ID, and while the woman cursed and fished through her purse, Mitchell told me that Clint tends to keep to himself but that Bo and Asa are a lot of fun.

I can't believe I'm hearing these things. I know people who have sat around with Tina, Cord, Nicki, Asa, and Clint. I'm getting closer, I can feel it.

This evening I was working as a Counter Elf at the Magic Tree when I saw a woman unzip her son's fly, release his penis, and instruct him to pee into a bank of artificial snow. He was a young child, four or five years old, and he did it, he peed. Urine dripped from the branches of artificial trees and puddled on the floor.

Tonight a man proposed to his girlfriend in one of the Santa houses. When Santa asked the man what he wanted for Christmas, he pulled a ring out of his pocket and said he wanted this woman to be his wife. Santa congratulated them both and the Photo Elf got choked up and started crying.

A spotted child visited Santa, climbed up on his lap, and expressed a wish to recover from chicken pox. Santa leapt up.

I've met elves from all walks of life. Most of them are show business people, actors and dancers, but a surprising number of them held real jobs at advertising agencies and brokerage firms before the recession hit. Bless their hearts, these people never imagined there was a velvet costume waiting in their future. They're the really bitter elves. Many of the elves are young, high school and college students. They're young and cute and one of the job perks is that I get to see them in their underpants. The changing rooms are located in the employee bathrooms behind SantaLand. The men's bathroom is small and the toilets often flood, so we are forced to stand on an island of newspapers in order to keep our socks dry. The Santas have a nice dressing room across the hall, but you don't want to see a Santa undress. Quite a few elves have taken to changing clothes in the hallway, beside their lockers. These elves tend to wear bathing suits underneath their costumes — jams, I believe they are called.

The overall cutest elf is a fellow from Queens named Snowball. Snowball tends to ham it up with the children, sometimes literally tumbling down the path to Santa's house. I tend to frown on that sort of behavior but Snowball is hands down adorable — you want to put him in your pocket. Yesterday we worked together as Santa Elves and I became excited when he started saying things like, "I'd follow *you* to Santa's house any day, Crumpet."

It made me dizzy, this flirtation.

By mid-afternoon I was running into walls. At the end of our shift we were in the bathroom, changing clothes, when suddenly we were surrounded by three Santas and five other elves — all of them were guys that Snowball had been flirting with.

Snowball just leads elves on, elves and Santas. He is playing a dangerous game.

This afternoon I was stuck being Photo Elf with Santa Santa. I don't know his real name; no one does. During most days, there is a slow period when you sit around the house and talk to your Santa. Most of them are nice guys and we sit around and laugh, but Santa Santa takes himself a bit too seriously. I asked him where he lives, Brooklyn or Manhattan, and he said, "Why, I live at the North Pole with Mrs. Claus!" I asked what he does the rest of the year and he said, "I make toys for all of the children."

I said, "Yes, but what do you do for money?"

"Santa doesn't need money," he said.

Santa Santa sits and waves and jingles his bell sash when no one is there. He actually recited "The Night Before Christmas," and it was just the two of us in the house, no children. Just us. What do you do with a nut like that?

He says, "Oh, Little Elf, Little Elf, straighten up those mantel toys for Santa." I reminded him that I have a name, Crumpet, and then I straightened up the stuffed animals.

"Oh, Little Elf, Little Elf, bring Santa a throat lozenge." So I brought him a lozenge.

Santa Santa has an elaborate little act for the children. He'll talk to them and give a hearty chuckle and ring his bells and then he asks them to name their favorite Christmas carol. Most of them say "Rudolph, the Red-Nosed Reindeer." Santa Santa then asks if they will sing it for him. The children are shy and don't want to sing out loud, so Santa Santa says, "Oh, Little Elf, Little Elf! Help young Brenda to sing that favorite carol of hers." Then I have to stand there and sing "Rudolph, the Red-Nosed Reindeer," which I hate. Half the time young Brenda's parents are my age and that certainly doesn't help matters much.

This afternoon I worked as an Exit Elf, telling people in a loud voice, "THIS WAY OUT OF SANTALAND." A woman was standing at one of the cash registers paying for her idea of a picture, while her son lay beneath her kicking and heaving, having a tantrum.

The woman said, "Riley, if you don't start behaving yourself, Santa's not going to bring you *any* of those toys you asked for."

The child said, "He is too going to bring me toys, liar, he already told me."

The woman grabbed my arm and said, "You there, Elf, tell Riley here that if he doesn't start behaving immediately, then Santa's going to change his mind and bring him coal for Christmas."

I said that Santa no longer traffics in coal. Instead, if you're bad he comes to your house and steals things. I told Riley that if he didn't behave himself, Santa was going to take away his TV and all his electrical appliances and leave him in the dark. "All your appliances, including the refrigerator. Your food is going to spoil and smell bad. It's going to be so cold and dark where you are. Man, Riley, are you ever going to suffer. You're going to wish you never heard the name Santa."

The woman got a worried look on her face and said, "All right, that's enough."

I said, "He's going to take your car and your furniture and all the towels and blankets and leave you with nothing."

The mother said, "No, that's enough, really."

I spend all day lying to people, saying, "You look so pretty," and, "Santa can't wait to visit with you. You're all he talks about. It's just not Christmas without you. You're Santa's favorite person in the entire tri-state area." Sometimes I lay it on real thick: "Aren't you the Princess of Rongovia? Santa said a beautiful Princess was coming here to visit him. He said she would be wearing a red dress and that she was very pretty, but not stuck up or two-faced. That's you, isn't it?" I lay it on and the parents mouth the words "Thank you" and "Good job."

To one child I said, "You're a model, aren't you?" The girl was maybe six years old and said, "Yes, I model, but I also act. I just got a second call-back for a Fisher Price commercial." The girl's mother said, "You may recognize Katelyn from the 'My First Sony' campaign. She's on the box." I said yes, of course.

All I do is lie, and that has made me immune to compliments.

Lately I am feeling trollish and have changed my elf name from Crumpet to Blisters. Blisters — I think it's cute.

Today a child told Santa Ken that he wanted his dead father back *and* a complete set of Teenage Mutant Ninja Turtles. Everyone wants those Turtles.

Last year a woman decided she wanted a picture of her cat sitting on Santa's lap, so she smuggled it into Macy's in a duffel bag. The cat sat on Santa's lap for five seconds before it shot out the door, and it took six elves forty-five minutes before they found it in the kitchen of the employee cafeteria.

A child came to Santa this morning and his mother said, "All right, Jason. Tell Santa what you want. Tell him what you want."

Jason said, "I . . . want . . . Prokton and . . . Gamble to . . . stop animal testing."

The mother said, "Proctor, Jason, that's Proctor and Gamble. And what do they do to animals? Do they torture animals, Jason? Is that what they do?"

Jason said, Yes, they torture. He was probably six years old.

This week my least favorite elf is a guy from Florida whom I call "The Walrus." The Walrus has a handlebar mustache, no chin, and a neck the size of my waist. In the dressing room he confesses to being "a bit of a ladies' man."

The Walrus acts as though SantaLand were a single's bar. It is embarrassing to work with him. We'll be together at the Magic Window, where he pulls women aside, places his arm around their shoulders, and says, "I know you're not going to ask Santa for good looks. You've already got those, pretty lady. Yes, you've got those in spades."

In his mind the women are charmed, dizzy with his attention.

I pull him aside and say, "That was a *mother* you just did that to, a married woman with three children."

He says, "I didn't see any ring." Then he turns to the next available woman and whistles, "Santa's married but I'm not. Hey, pretty lady, I've got plenty of room on my knee."

I Photo Elfed all day for a variety of Santas and it struck me that many of the parents don't allow their children to speak at all. A child sits upon Santa's lap and the parents say, "All right now, Amber, tell Santa what you want. Tell him you want a Baby Alive and My Pretty Ballerina and that winter coat you saw in the catalog."

The parents name the gifts they have already bought. They don't want to hear the word "pony," or "television set," so they talk through the entire visit, placing words in the child's mouth. When the child hops off the lap, the parents address their children, each and every time, with, "What do you say to Santa?"

The child says, "Thank you, Santa."

It is sad because you would like to believe that everyone is unique and then they disappoint you every time by being exactly the same, asking for the same things, reciting the exact same lines as though they have been handed a script.

All of the adults ask for a Gold Card or a BMW and they rock with laughter, thinking they are the first person brazen enough to request such pleasures.

Santa says, "I'll see what I can do."

Couples over the age of fifty all say, "I don't want to sit on your lap, Santa, I'm afraid I might break it!"

How do you break a lap? How did so many people get the idea to say the exact same thing?

I went to a store on the Upper West Side. This store is like a Museum of Natural History where everything is for sale: every taxidermic or skeletal animal that roams the earth is represented in this shop and, because of that, it is popular. I went with my brother last weekend. Near the cash register was a bowl of glass eyes and a sign reading "DO NOT HOLD THESE GLASS EYES UP AGAINST YOUR OWN EYES: THE ROUGH STEM CAN CAUSE INJURY."

I talked to the fellow behind the counter and he said, "It's the same thing every time. First they hold up the eyes and then they go for the horns. I'm sick of it."

It frightened me that, until I saw the sign, my first impulse was to hold those eyes up to my own. I thought it might be a laugh riot.

All of us take pride and pleasure in the fact that we are unique, but I'm afraid that when all is said and done the police are right: it all comes down to fingerprints.

There was a big "Sesame Street Live" extravaganza over at Madison Square Garden, so thousands of people decided to make a day of it and go straight from Sesame Street to Santa. We were packed today, absolutely packed, and everyone was cranky. Once the line gets long we break it up into four different lines because anyone in their right mind would leave if they

knew it would take over two hours to see Santa. Two hours —
you could see a movie in two hours. Standing in a two-hour line
makes people worry that they're not living in a democratic nation. People stand in line for two hours and they go over the
edge. I was sent into the hallway to direct the second phase of
the line. The hallway was packed with people, and all of them
seemed to stop me with a question: which way to the down escalator, which way to the elevator, the Patio Restaurant, gift
wrap, the women's rest room, Trim-A-Tree. There was a line for
Santa and a line for the women's bathroom, and one woman,
after asking me a dozen questions already, asked, "Which is the
line for the women's bathroom?" I shouted that I thought it was
the line with all the women in it.

She said, "I'm going to have you fired."

I had two people say that to me today, "I'm going to have you
fired." Go ahead, be my guest. I'm wearing a green velvet costume; it doesn't get any worse than this. Who do these people
think they are?

"I'm going to have you fired!" and I wanted to lean over and
say, "I'm going to have you killed."

In the Maze, on the way to Santa's house, you pass
spectacles — train sets, dancing bears, the candy-cane forest,
and the penguins. The penguins are set in their own icy wonderland. They were built years ago and they frolic mechani-
cally. They stand outside their igloo and sled and skate and fry
fish in a pan. For some reason people feel compelled to throw
coins into the penguin display. I can't figure it out for the life
of me — they don't throw money at the tree of gifts or the mechanical elves, or the mailbox of letters, but they empty their
pockets for the penguins. I asked what happens to that money,
and a manager told me that it's collected for charity, but I don't
think so. Elves take the quarters for the pay phone, housekeep-
ing takes the dimes, and I've seen visitors, those that aren't
throwing money, I've seen them scooping it up as fast as they
can.

I was working the Exit today. I'm supposed to say, "This way *out* of SantaLand," but I can't bring myself to say it as it seems like I'm rushing people. They wait an hour to see Santa, they're hit up for photo money, and then someone's hustling them out. I say, "This way *out* of SantaLand if you've decided maybe it's time for you to go home."

"You can exit this way if you feel like it."

We're also supposed to encourage people to wait outside while the parent with money is paying for a picture. "If you're waiting for someone to purchase a photo, wait *outside* the double doors."

I say, "If you're waiting for someone to purchase a picture, you might want to wait *outside* the double doors where it is pleasant and the light is more flattering."

I had a group of kids waiting this afternoon, waiting for their mom to pay for pictures, and this kid reached into his pocket and threw a nickel at me. He was maybe twelve years old, jaded in regard to Santa, and he threw his nickel and it hit my chest and fell to the floor. I picked it up, cleared my throat, and handed it back to him. He threw it again. Like I was a penguin. So I handed it back and he threw it higher, hitting me in the neck. I picked up the nickel and turned to another child and said, "Here, you dropped this." He examined the coin, put it in his pocket, and left.

Yesterday was my day off, and the afflicted came to visit Santa. I Photo Elfed for Santa Ira this afternoon, and he told me all about it. These were severely handicapped children who arrived on stretchers and in wheelchairs. Santa couldn't put them on his lap, and often he could not understand them when they voiced their requests. He made it a point to grab each child's hand and ask what they wanted for Christmas. He did this until he came to a child who had no hands. This made him self-conscious, so he started placing a hand on the child's knee until he came to a child with no legs. After that he decided to simply nod his head and chuckle.

*   *   *

I got stuck with Santa Santa again this afternoon and had to sing and fetch for three hours. Late in the afternoon, a child said she didn't know what her favorite Christmas carol was. Santa said, "'Rudolph'? 'Jingle Bells'? 'White Christmas'? 'Here Comes Santa Claus'? 'Away in the Manger'? 'Silent Night'?"

The girl agreed to "Away in the Manger," but didn't want to sing it because she didn't know the words.

Santa Santa said, "Oh, Little Elf, Little Elf, come sing 'Away in the Manger' for us."

It didn't seem fair that I should have to solo, so I told him I didn't know the words.

Santa Santa said, "Of course you know the words. Come now, sing!"

So I sang it the way Billie Holiday might have sung it if she'd put out a Christmas album. "Away in the manger, no crib for a bed, the little Lord, Jesus, lay down his sweet head."

Santa Santa did not allow me to finish.

This afternoon we set a record by scooting fourteen hundred people through SantaLand in the course of an hour. Most of them were school groups in clots of thirty or more. My Santa would address them, saying, "All right, I'm going to count to three, and on three I want you all to yell what you want and I need you to say it as loud as you can."

Then he would count to three and the noise was magnificent. Santa would cover his ears and say, "All right — one by one I want you to tell me what you're planning to leave Santa on Christmas Eve."

He would go around the room and children would name different sorts of cookies, and he would say, "What about sandwiches? What if Santa should want something more substantial than a cookie?"

Santa's thrust this afternoon was the boredom of his nine-year relationship. He would wave the children good-bye and then turn to me, saying, "I want an affair, Goddamn it — just a little one, just something to get me through the next four or five years."

＊ ＊ ＊

Some of these children, they get nervous just before going in to visit Santa. They pace and wring their hands and stare at the floor. They act like they're going in for a job interview. I say, "Don't worry, Santa's not going to judge you. He's very relaxed about that sort of thing. He used to be judgmental but people gave him a hard time about it so he stopped. Trust me, you have nothing to worry about."

I was Photo Elf tonight for the oldest Santa. Usually their names are written on the water cups they keep hidden away on the toy shelf. Every now and then a Santa will call out for water and an elf will hold the cup while his master drinks through a straw. I looked on the cup and saw no name. We were busy tonight and I had no time for an introduction. This was an outstanding Santa, wild but warm. The moment a family leaves, this Santa, sensing another group huddled upon his doorstep, will begin to sing.

He sings, "A pretty girl . . . is like a melody."

The parents and children enter the room, and if there is a girl in the party, Santa will take a look at her, hold his gloved hands to his chest, and fake a massive heart attack — falling back against the cushion and moaning with a combination of pleasure and pain. Then he slowly comes out of it and says, "Elf, Elf . . . are you there?"

"Yes, Santa, I'm here."

"Elf, I just had a dream that I was standing before the most beautiful girl in the world. She was right here, in my house."

Then I say, "It wasn't a dream, Santa. Open your eyes, my friend. She's standing before you."

Santa rubs his eyes and shakes his head as if he were a parish priest, visited by Christ. "Oh, heavenly day," he says, addressing the child. "You are *the* most beautiful girl I have seen in six hundred and seventeen years."

Then he scoops her into his lap and flatters every aspect of her character. The child is delirious. Santa gestures toward the girl's mother, asking, "Is that your sister I see standing there in the corner?"

"No, that's my mother."

Santa calls the woman over close and asks if she has been a good mother. "Do you tell your daughter that you love her? Do you tell her every day?"

The mothers always blush and say, "I try, Santa."

Santa asks the child to give her mother a kiss. Then he addresses the father, again requesting that he tell the child how much he loves her.

Santa ends the visit, saying, "Remember that the most important thing is to try and love other people as much as they love you."

The parents choke up and often cry. They grab Santa's hand and, on the way out, my hand. They say it was worth the wait. The most severe cases open their wallets and hand Santa a few bucks. We're not supposed to accept tips, but most Santas take the money and wink, tucking it into their boot. This Santa looked at the money as if it were a filthy Kleenex. He closed his eyes and prepared for the next family.

With boys, this Santa plays on their brains: each one is the smartest boy in the world.

The great thing about this Santa is that he never even asks what the children want. Most times he involves the parents to the point where they surrender their urge for documentation. They lay down their video recorders and gather round for the festival of love.

I was the Pointer Elf again this afternoon, one of my favorite jobs. The Pointer stands inside the Magic Tree and appoints available Santa Elves to lead parties of visitors to the houses. First-time visitors are enthusiastic, eager that they are moments away from Santa. Some of the others, having been here before, have decided to leave nothing to chance.

Out of all the Santas, two are black and both are so light-skinned that, with the beard and makeup, you would be hard-pressed to determine their race.

Last week, a black woman became upset when, having requested a "Santa of color," she was sent to Jerome.

After she was led to the house, the woman returned to the Pointer and demanded to speak with a manager.

"He's not black," the woman complained.

Bridget assured this woman that Jerome was indeed black.

The woman said, "Well, he isn't black enough."

Jerome is a difficult Santa, moody and unpredictable. He spends a lot of time staring off into space and tallying up his paycheck for the hours he has worked so far. When a manager ducks in encouraging him to speed things up, Jerome says, "Listen up, I'm playing a role here. Do you understand? A dramatic role that takes a great deal of preparation, so don't hassle me about 'Time.' "

Jerome seems to have his own bizarre agenda. When the children arrive, he looks down at his boots and lectures them, suggesting a career in entomology.

"Entomology, do you know what that is?"

He tells them that the defensive spray of the stink bug may contain medicinal powers that can one day cure mankind of communicable diseases.

"Do you know about holistic medicine?" he asks.

The Photo Elf takes a picture of yawning children.

The other black Santa works during weeknights and I have never met him but hear he is a real entertainer, popular with Photo Elves and children.

The last time I was the Pointer Elf, a woman approached me and whispered, "We would like a *traditional* Santa. I'm sure you know what I'm talking about."

I sent her to Jerome.

Yesterday Snowball was the Pointer and a woman pulled him aside, saying, "Last year we had a chocolate Santa. Make sure it doesn't happen again."

I saw it all today. I was Pointer Elf for all of five minutes before a man whispered, "Make sure we get a white one this year. Last year we were stuck with a black."

A woman touched my arm and mouthed, "White — white like *us.*"

I address a Santa Elf, the first in line, and hand these people over. Who knows where they will wind up? The children are antsy, excited — they want to see Santa. The children are sweet. The parents are manipulative and should be directed toward the A&S Plaza, two blocks away. A&S has only two Santas working at the same time — a white Santa and a black Santa, and it's very clear-cut: whites in one line and blacks in another.

I've had requests from both sides. White Santa, black Santa, a Pointer Elf is instructed to shrug his shoulders and feign ignorance, saying, "There's only one Santa."

Today I experienced my cash register nightmare. The actual financial transactions weren't so bad — I've gotten the hang of that. The trouble are the voids. A customer will offer to pay in cash and then, after I have arranged it, they examine their wallets and say, "You know what, I think I'll put that on my card instead."

This involves voids and signatures from the management.

I take care of the paperwork, accept their photo form and staple it to the receipt. Then it is my job to say, "The pictures taken today will be mailed January twelfth."

The best part of the job is watching their faces fall. These pictures are sent to a lab to be processed; it takes time, all these pictures so late in the season. If they wanted their pictures to arrive before Christmas, they should have come during the first week we were open. Lots of people want their money back after learning the pictures will arrive after Christmas, in January, when Christmas is forgotten. Void.

We were very crowded today and I got a kick out of completing the transaction, handing the customer a receipt, and saying, "Your photos will be mailed on August tenth."

August is much funnier than January. I just love to see that look on someone's face, the mouth a perfect O.

* * *

This was my last day of work. We had been told that Christmas Eve is a slow day, but this was the day a week of training was meant to prepare us for. It was a day of nonstop action, a day when the managers spent a great deal of time with their walkie-talkies.

I witnessed a fistfight between two mothers and watched while a woman experienced a severe, crowd-related anxiety attack: falling to the floor and groping for breath, her arms moving as though she were fighting off bats. A Long Island father called Santa a faggot because he couldn't take the time to recite "The Night Before Christmas" to his child. Parents in long lines left disposable diapers at the door to Santa's house. It was the rowdiest crowd I have ever seen, and we were short on elves, many of whom simply did not show up or called in sick. As a result we had our lunch hours cut in half and had to go without our afternoon breaks. Many elves complained bitterly, but the rest of us found ourselves in the moment we had all been waiting for. It was us against them. It was time to be a trouper, and I surrendered completely. My Santa and I had them on the lap, off the lap in forty-five seconds flat. We were an efficient machine surrounded by chaos. Quitting time came and went for the both of us and we paid it no mind. My plane was due to leave at eight o'clock, and I stayed until the last moment, figuring the time it would take to get to the airport. It was with reservation that I reported to the manager, telling her I had to leave. She was at a cash register, screaming at a customer. She was, in fact, calling this customer a bitch. I touched her arm and said, "I have to go now." She laid her hand on my shoulder, squeezed it gently, and continued her conversation, saying, "Don't tell the store president I called you a bitch. Tell him I called you a fucking bitch, because that's exactly what you are. Now get out of my sight before I do something we both regret."